"Not just a quick-fix self-help book, *What Makes You Stronger* provides a manual for crafting a more fulfilling life through awareness and values-based action. Based on solid behavioral science as well as uncommon wisdom, this book invites the reader to discover sources of wellness both within and without."

—**Richard M. Ryan, PhD**, clinical psychologist, professor at the Institute for Positive Psychology and Education at Australian Catholic University, and cofounder of self-determination theory

"Practical, fun, and comprehensive—this book will provide you with all the tools you need to navigate the complexities and curveballs that life may throw at you. I'd highly recommend getting a copy and diving into the wisdom that is set out in these pages."

—**Joe Oliver, PhD**, founder of Contextual Consulting, associate professor at University College London, and coauthor of *The Mindfulness and Acceptance Workbook for Self-Esteem*

"This book is truly empowering. Beautifully packed with wise, manageable strategies for living with strength and purpose. It takes you through a compassionate journey that invites you to dream big—to step outside of your comfort zone and build resistance, vitality, as well as meaningful connections. This book teaches you that you are strong enough to carry both fear and uncertainty in building the life you want to live."

—**Rikke Kjelgaard**, licensed psychologist, author, speaker, acceptance and commitment therapy (ACT) expert, and chief rock'n'roller and passionate changemaker at www.rikkekjelgaard.com

"Written in a highly accessible, practical style, *What Makes You Stronger* provides a simple set of steps you can take to pursue the life you've always dreamed of having, but perhaps felt you were not strong enough or worthy enough to make it so. As this book beautifully demonstrates, you have at your fingertips all the tools needed to weather life's unpredictable moments, and at the same time to bond with yourself and the people and things that matter to you in the world. Highly recommended!"

—**Kirk Strosahl, PhD**, cofounder of ACT, and coauthor of *The Mindfulness and Acceptance Workbook for Depression*

T0000744

"Do you sometimes feel that you are living like a zombie, just mindlessly responding to the many demands placed on you? Do you sometimes feel disconnected from your values and your destination? *What Makes You Stronger* teaches you concrete skills that allow you to become a stronger self and to make stronger social connections. Louise Hayes, Joseph Ciarrochi, and Ann Bailey have produced an approachable and easy-to-read text that will guide you through your life. I highly recommend it."

> **—Stefan G. Hofmann, PhD**, Alexander von Humboldt professor at Philipps University of Marburg in Germany, and coauthor of *Learning Process-Based Therapy*

"I opened the pages of *What Makes You Stronger* and instantly fell in love! Louise Hayes, Joseph Ciarrochi, and Ann Bailey have hit a home run! The engaging work found in this self-help book about creating a purposeful life by building vulnerability, awareness, love, friendship, and flexibility sits right at the feet of vitality. The illustrations are amazing! I can only imagine that each person who reads this work will do nothing but grow, finding their path to meaningful living."

> **—Robyn D. Walser, PhD**, licensed clinical psychologist, author of *The Heart of ACT*, and coauthor of *The Mindful Couple*, *Learning ACT II*, *The ACT Workbook for Anger*, and *ACT for Moral Injury*

"The DNA-V model is an accessible and memorable way to think about some of the core processes of change that we know are important to psychological health. If you can learn to be more psychologically flexible, your life will change. Like a flashlight on a pathway, this book will help make that journey clearer."

> **—Steven C. Hayes**, originator of ACT, and author of *A Liberated Mind*

"This book speaks to all of us who have felt lost, hopeless, or like we're simply not enough. It helps develop and strengthen fundamental abilities to develop a meaningful life, abandon useless battles with our own thoughts and feelings, and turn pain into fuel to pursue our deepest longing in life. A must-read also for clinical psychologists.... And, by the way, it has a strong scientific base, too."

> **—Giovambattista Presti, MD, PhD**, professor of psychology at University of Enna Kore in Italy, and past president of the Association for Contextual Behavioral Science

WHAT
MAKES
YOU
STRONGER

How to Thrive in the Face of Change and Uncertainty Using Acceptance and Commitment Therapy

Louise L. Hayes, PhD
Joseph V. Ciarrochi, PhD
Ann Bailey, MPsych

New Harbinger Publications, Inc.

Publisher's Note

This publication is designed to provide accurate and authoritative information in regard to the subject matter covered. It is sold with the understanding that the publisher is not engaged in rendering psychological, financial, legal, or other professional services. If expert assistance or counseling is needed, the services of a competent professional should be sought.

NEW HARBINGER PUBLICATIONS is a registered trademark of New Harbinger Publications, Inc.

New Harbinger Publications is an employee-owned company.

Copyright © 2022 by Louise L. Hayes, Joseph V. Ciarrochi, and Ann Bailey
New Harbinger Publications, Inc.
5674 Shattuck Avenue
Oakland, CA 94609
www.newharbinger.com

All Rights Reserved

Illustrations by Katharine Hall

Interior layout and design by Catherine Adam / Wonderbird Photography and Design Studio
www.wonderbird.nz

Cover design by Catherine Adam and Katharine Hall

Acquired by Tesilya Hanauer

Edited by Karen Levy

Library of Congress Cataloging-in-Publication Data on file

Printed in the United States of America

24   23   22

10   9   8   7   6   5   4   3   2   1   First Printing

To my brothers, Jeff, Ian, and John, thank you for making me laugh often.

To Jackson, Darcy, and Alana, thank you for cherishing our family.

As always, for life with Mingma: Nga chenbu chegee khorla.
—LLH

To Grace, Vincent, and Ann, thank you for filling my life with energy and purpose.
—JVC

To my parents, Helen and Grahame; my brother Grant; and my universe, Joseph, Grace, and Vincent. Thank you for your love.
—AB

ACKNOWLEDGMENTS

Creating a book such as this requires the work of many. We would like to extend our sincere gratitude to the following people: Katharine Hall from www.kathallcreative.com, for making our words come alive in your illustrations; Catherine Adam from www.wonderbird.nz, for inspiring the design, inside and out; our editors, Tesilya Hanauer and Vicraj Gill, for their guidance on early drafts; Karen Levy, for copyediting; and all of the staff at New Harbinger. Thank you to our early beta readers, Louise Whiting, Alana Ray, Jackson Hayes, and Darcy Hayes.

This work would not exist without the original ACT work written by Steve Hayes, Kirk Strosahl, and Kelly Wilson, and the ongoing support and connection with the community at the Association for Contextual Behavioral Science.

And finally, to colleagues and friends for their encouragement, support, and, most of all, patience over the writing years. Thank you for being there when we call for help. We are blessed with so many wonderful people who use DNA-V in their work and the many clients who share their lives with us—each of you makes the hard work of writing this next advance on DNA-V well worth it.

CONTENTS

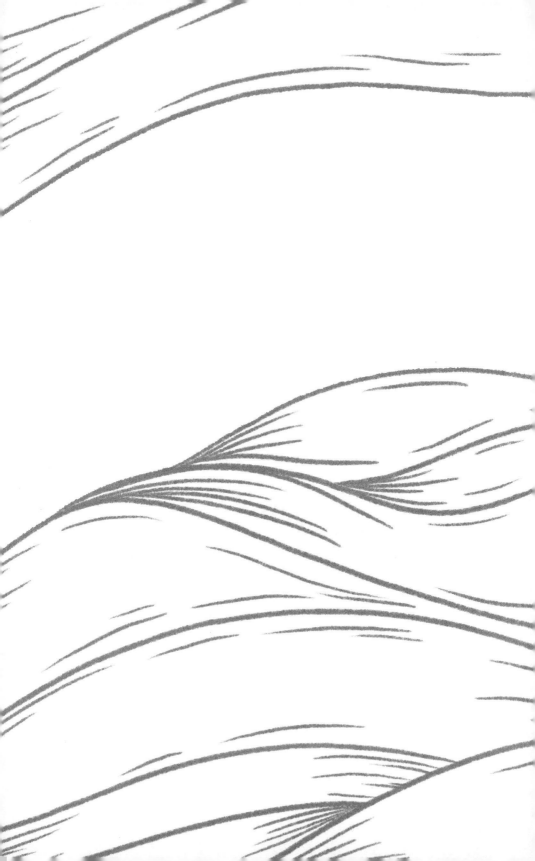

DNA-V: THE FOUR FOUNDATIONS OF PSYCHOLOGICAL STRENGTH

Once you realize change and control are incompatible, you are set free.

Changes in your life can be constant and disorienting. You want your life to be predictable. You want your world to be predictable, too. But it isn't. Life is hard. You'll face almost constant uncertainty and struggle. However, you can learn to live with purpose, even in the face of changes. Here you will learn a science-based way to live flexibly no matter what the world throws at you. Change can make you stronger.

We'll give you an overview of this book here by following a case study of Dawa. She's a newly graduated young lawyer, setting out for her dream job. After years of study and hard work, she lands a job with a high-profile law firm. Dawa soon realizes the dream job isn't as she imagined. Her boss is a bully. She criticizes Dawa in meetings, creates alliances against her, allocates pointless tasks, and withholds important information. Dawa responds by being efficient and polite, hoping her boss will like her. She also doubles down on her old strategies of working harder and developing an inner toughness. Dawa pounds herself with criticisms: *Get tougher, you weakling.* Her boss feeds on power and Dawa's attempts to play nice only makes things worse. Dawa suspects her boss is trying to make her crack. The pressure is oddly familiar, too; it's reminiscent of that teacher who bullied her so badly the school fired him. A thought creeps in sometimes that maybe *it's her*; maybe there's something wrong with *her*.

But she can't dwell. She's effectively got two jobs now—her paid employment plus her self-imposed job of controlling her feelings and thoughts. She works so hard that she eventually burns out. Control of her thoughts and feelings gives her the illusion that she's coping, but the sheer effort leaves her spinning.

Controlling change means you try to stop things that can't be stopped. For this lawyer, that is a bad boss *and* a lost dream job. Her strategies are based on controlling it all: internal strategies like being tough on herself, and external ones like making endless to-do lists, always having her files in order, and even wearing lucky socks. Nothing she does can control her boss's mood. Nor can she stop her distressful thoughts and feelings. They make sense here; she *should* be feeling overwhelmed if she's bullied. Dawa must find another way.

This book offers you a radical premise: Trying to control the wrong things brings loss of control. If you try to control how you think and feel, how other people think and feel, or how external events unfold, you'll lose control. You'll lose the very life you are trying to protect. You'll get stuck. You need a different way to respond to changes. In this book, you'll learn to face change with courage and hope instead of resisting it. Then, and only then, will change make you stronger.

What to Expect in This Book

This book will show you how to build inner flexibility so that you can grow from struggles. Flexibility is the opposite of control; it's learning to bend with the wind so that you don't break. This book will provide a simple, practical system built from effective research. We call the system DNA-V[1]. We've grounded DNA-V in evidence-based approaches from acceptance and commitment therapy,[2] positive psychology,[3] process-based therapy,[4] mindfulness-based interventions,[5] self-determination theory,[6] adult attachment theory,[7] and evolutionary science.[8] Ultimately, what distinguishes this book from many other self-help books is our deep commitment to science and research. Wisdom traditions of the past also influence us, especially when linked to the latest research evidence. The book is highly referenced; if you're interested, you can look up the evidence as you read.

In part 1, we explain the core abilities of the DNA-V system. In part 2, we apply those abilities to expanding and strengthening the self, and then in part 3, we further expand the abilities to your social world. Think of a stone being dropped in water and the small ripples expanding to big ripples. Similarly, you will gradually learn to expand your life, from inner skills to outer world. Here's a brief snapshot on what's inside.

Part 1: The DNA-V System

The DNA-V system has four core abilities that we call discoverer, noticer, advisor, and valuer. Developing each of these abilities can make you stronger, more able to adapt to change and build purpose in your life. The first four chapters cover each ability in detail. There is no correct order to use the abilities or learn about them. With our example of Dawa, she's trapped with her advisor, so we begin there and will show you the DNA-V model following the order most useful for her.

Your Advisor Allows You to Master Your Thinking

Your *advisor* is a science-informed concept. We use it to show you how thoughts work, and how to build a flexible cognitive style. Flexibility means that you use thoughts in helpful ways, and either try new thinking strategies or shift to another DNA-V ability when you're stuck. For example, if you are overthinking, ruminating, or following unhelpful beliefs, you can learn to let that thinking go and shift to embracing the present moment (noticer) or shift to taking action to find a new way forward (discoverer).

Pop psychology has likely taught you that strength comes from having positive thoughts. You see this in books like *Awaken the Giant Within* and *The Power of Positive Thinking*. Their core idea is that you can reject uncertainty by creating positive thoughts and convincing yourself you are strong. This gives you the life you want. That concept has failed miserably. If it succeeded, we'd all be doing it and living happily ever after. We'd only need one book telling us to think positively, not a thousand. In this book we are going to propose something very different.

> Strength is not the ability to think positively.
> It's the ability to use thinking, positive and negative,
> to build a better life.

Dawa is trying hard to think positively, but it isn't working. She is in a toxic workplace telling herself to stay strong. That's like being gnawed by a rat while contemplating how sunny the day is. It's time for something radically different. When she develops her advisor ability, she'll know that trying to force herself to be positive will fail. Instead, she'll learn how to turn her thinking energy into a flexible style that helps her problem solve, predict how people will act, motivate herself, and take a wider perspective. Her thoughts are her supercomputer, and the DNA-V approach will help her get the bugs out of her programming.

Your Noticer Builds Inner Wisdom and Outer Calm

Noticing is in the moments of life. Noticing is within your body and includes your ability to experience life through your five senses and feelings. Your body is a sensitive instrument, able to rapidly detect threat and opportunity. It carries both joy and stress—moments when your heart sings with a hug or sinks after receiving bad news.

Just as our culture may promote positive thoughts, it may also promote only positive emotions, telling us to accentuate the positive and eliminate the negative. We will show you that your attempts to control negative feelings only create more negative feelings. You can get stuck trying to hold back your negative feelings with destructive strategies like avoiding feelings or falling into unhealthy habits. You'll see your noticer ability can help you gain presence and purpose. You can learn to respond wisely, to manage emotions, and to care for your physical self. If you are willing to open to the vulnerability, you'll be able to expand your life.

> Strength isn't controlling fear; strength is making space for fear and responding wisely.

Dawa thinks she is a failure because she feels afraid and insecure. When she uses her noticer ability wisely, she'll learn how to acknowledge her hurt and know that feeling unsafe isn't a weakness. Her noticing will tell her that she is in a toxic environment and that she needs to act. From her quiet awareness, she'll gain power. She'll discover that she is flexible enough to hold her fear and still act effectively.

Your Discoverer: A Bridge to Your Better Self

Your *discoverer* helps you leave your comfort zone and do something new so that you learn and grow within yourself and your social world. You can use your discoverer when old strategies and habits aren't working. Changing old patterns of behavior can be tough. First, because change brings uncertainty, *we avoid it*. For example, people stay in unfulfilling friendships because they fear it's too hard to pull back or make new friends. Second, change can threaten our *sense of competence*. People stay in boring jobs because they can't imagine what a different career path would look like. Third, change can make us feel *others are controlling us*. We get resentful and push back. For example, people hate when governments change the way things are done and they can't justify the reason. Finally, change is resisted because it is *effortful*. We might make the decision to stay in our current boring job because job searching is hard. The final way we resist change is to close our minds by *assuming our predictions are right*, and that we *know our limitations* and cannot make a change. Then we relinquish hope.

From the outside, we can see how Dawa is stuck with the comfortable discomfort of her habits. She's worked hard to get through law school by pushing herself. Pushing herself once helped her, but now it makes things worse. It is hard for her to let go of a strategy that has worked so well in the past. When she engages her discoverer ability, she'll learn how to see her problem with new eyes and new strategies.

> Strength requires the courage to let go of the old and discover a new way forward, a bridge to a better self.

Your Valuer Directs Your Life Toward Purpose

Your discoverer, noticer, and advisor are abilities that you can use to build value in your life. This brings us to your *valuer*, which has two components: *Valued action* is your ability to take purposeful steps; *vitality* is your ability to bring energy and engagement into your day. The goal of this book is to help you bring more purpose and energy into your life.

Commitment ceremonies have valued purpose *and* vital energy. Have you ever cried when witnessing a loving couple give their vows? That joyful moment symbolizes how central value is to you, but also illustrates that value comes with a companion—vulnerability. Just like you, this couple's joy today will not last; they will work for happiness but also know sadness. Like you, this couple will face change over and over. They will age, perhaps grow apart, maybe grow closer. If they build their life on value instead of on an idealized way that relationships should be, they have a chance to grow stronger each year. If they hide or suppress their vulnerable feelings, they might grow apart.

> Strength requires you to be open to value and allow vulnerability.

Dawa faces a difficult choice. A valued choice is to honor her longing for fulfillment within herself and her career. This will make her feel vulnerable because she cares, not because she is weak. An alternative is to turn away; in doing so, the bully forces her to give up her life. With values as her guide, she'll be clear which choice to make. She'll grow strong. Values will become her shield.

> Strength requires you to flexibly shift between discoverer, noticer, and advisor to create value and vitality. Strength is change.

Part 2: Strengthening the Self

Chapters 5 through 9 will show you how to strengthen your DNA-V abilities to become a stronger self, one that can grow beyond false limitations. You'll take a deep dive into who you *think* you are and will emerge capable and grounded, able to be vulnerable, boundless, compassionate, achieving, and profoundly aware of your presence in the world.

Vulnerable is to know that your embodied self and emotions are an essential part of you, a crucial way to experience life and other people. *Boundless* is to see yourself as unlimited, to know that you need not be trapped by words and labels, like *not smart enough*, or *not good enough*. *Compassionate* is to open yourself to courage and kindness. *Achieving* is to set yourself toward growth by strengthening your abilities and working for your highest goals. *Profound awareness* is where you learn how to train your mind and body to become an open, grounded presence, living with all your heart and connecting with the world.

Dawa has spent a decade in law school, but all the facts and case law did not teach her how to face change from within. Through these chapters on strengthening the self, she can come to understand that her shattered dream is not a personal fault. She can learn that attacking herself with criticism is futile, but building a strong, compassionate presence is impenetrable.

Building Stronger Social Connections

The final four chapters expand into your social world. Here you'll consider how others bring change to you, and what you can do about that. We'll show you how to let go of unhelpful patterns, face changing relationships, deal with difficulties with other people, and work toward more love and connection. Then, in the final chapter, you will see how all your DNA-V abilities can come together to help you live even while the world delivers constant and often frightening changes. Fueled by your value, you will learn how to use your DNA-V abilities to adapt. Where there is hopelessness, DNA-V brings you active hope.

Dawa is shaken by her changing social world. She anticipated a rewarding career, but is stuck in a toxic workplace. The bullying has triggered past social difficulties. Every chapter in this social section will give her insights into her social actions and then help her get loose from unworkable habits such as avoidance, acquiescence, and self-blame. She'll learn how to be effectively assertive so that she can build her career. And she'll learn how to strengthen her close relationships to receive and give love and support.

Dawa's situation isn't unique, but it does show how the DNA-V system can help people reimagine their life. Later in the book, you'll read stories about how other people used the DNA-V system to handle difficult situations.

Dawa's life can be transformed.

Your life can be transformed, too.

Part 1

YOUR FOUNDATION FOR CHANGE

When you use all your DNA-V abilities,
your walk of life is paved with purpose.

You are now ready to learn how to maximize your abilities in ways that will help you face change and grow stronger. In the introduction, we gave you a brief overview of the parts of the system, just so you could see them all together. You already have D, N, A, and V abilities within you. Now we take a deeper dive into how you can use these four abilities in life. Some ways you use them now might be getting you stuck, but if you change how you use them, you can become stronger. In these four chapters, we'll help you learn to spot this distinction between growing stronger and becoming stuck.

The disk illustration is one way of thinking about yourself and how you can face change. Let's move between the abilities now to see how easy it is to apply the DNA-V system to something important in your life.

Begin by thinking about your relationships and identify someone you value but with whom you are often in conflict. Maybe you argue or disagree often.

Move into *advisor* space

Take a moment to think about the conflict you have. What is causing it? What are you thinking when you are in the conflict? What should you do about it? This is using your advisor. You are problem solving and figuring things out.

Move to your *noticer* space

Now, take a few slow breaths (not deep, just slow). Don't rush. Give yourself a moment to breathe. Notice what is happening inside you. You are using your noticer when you are experiencing the world through your body and senses, such as when you are immersed in nature or absorbed in a conversation with a friend. Now, let your mind drift to the conflict, and notice how the conflict feels in your body. Do you notice tension anywhere? What feelings do you carry in your body? Anger, stress, sadness? Notice what it feels like to have conflict with that person. Now shift your noticing to the outside world by sensing what is around you. Slow down. Notice any smells, sights, or sounds. You have just connected with your noticer; take a moment to be aware of what it feels like.

Move to your *discoverer* space

You are using your discoverer well when you're interacting with the world and open to feedback. When you do something new, you grow; when you stay in your comfort zone, you don't. Think again about that conflict. How do you typically act when in conflict? Do you argue, raise your voice, go cold? Be aware of your typical action strategy and how it works. Now think about doing something new or unusual in that conflict. What new behavior might you try? Doing something new might feel uncomfortable too.

Move to your *valuing* center

We put value and vitality in the middle of your DNA-V disk. Imagine you can turn your valuing toward your discoverer, noticer, or advisor ability, depending on what is important to you. Let's say you value improving your relationship and reducing conflict. Then that determines how you direct your energy. Will thinking about the situation help you reduce conflict? Then use your advisor ability. Will you benefit from slowing down, pausing, and not reacting to feelings? Then use your noticer ability. Finally, would you like to do something new in this relationship and see whether it improves the conflict? Then use your discoverer ability.

With the DNA-V system, you are able to rapidly change in the space of just a few minutes, between doing things in your relationship (D), noticing your feelings in the relationship (N), and thinking about your relationship (A). Isn't that amazing? You are always moving, even if you don't notice it. The DNA-V disk illustrates how you are constant change. You'll never stop yearning, never stop caring; you're always moving to engage all your abilities to help you love your life.

Now it is time to begin your DNA-V journey. We could start anywhere in the DNA-V model, but our first chapter will start at your center: your valuer. Once you know your value, then you will have a pathway to growth and change, and you will have purpose behind your strength.

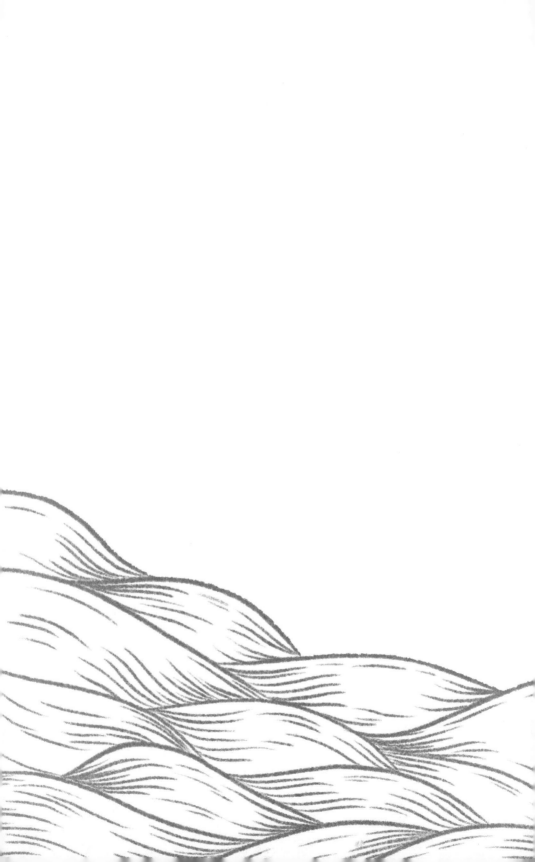

 **Chapter 1**

VALUER:
DIRECTS YOUR LIFE
TOWARD PURPOSE

Let your heart guide your life. Ask yourself each day: *What matters most?* You may not know the answer, but you can search for it. The search will transform you.

n still moments, you might question the profoundness of your life, asking whether you are making your life count or just making it through. Perhaps this moment comes as you walk in nature absorbed by the strength of trees that have stood longer than you. Here you can be still enough to sense your longing for something more. The busyness of everyday life has quietened. Only forest and you. You feel the urge for more life. Each day, week, month, and year brings new challenges, making it hard to stop and hear that longing. *What do I want in my life? What do I need?* In that quiet, you might also hear pain. *I want it to be easier. I just want to live peacefully, to be happy and have love. That's not too much to ask, is it?* That can be hard to listen to. Regret fills the quiet. Perhaps you've lost life to habit—get up, work, sleep, repeat, a never-ending cycle.

Make these quiet moments matter. Know that you are not alone in this struggle; we are all interconnected in the very same struggle. In this chapter, we invite you to spend some time connecting with your meaning and purpose. You will see why listening to your longing matters, why it comes with struggle, and how listening makes you stronger.

What most people long for is vitality and value. Vitality is the extent you feel *alive, energetic,* and *engaged,* like when laughing with a friend or enthusiastically embracing new challenges. Value refers to what is in your heart, what is personally important to you in the long term. Valued actions might include connecting with others, challenging yourself and learning, being physically active, being spiritual, giving to others, embracing the moment, and caring for yourself.[1] Values are not what you *think,* but what you *do;* that's why we call it valued action. Values are something you work toward; you take valued action now for a future outcome. When you start looking at what you value, you start knowing what is worth fighting for. If you don't look, nothing changes.

....

A Tale of Two Worlds

You are about to experience two worlds by imagining that you live in the places we describe below. Notice what happens within your body and mind as you read.

Day One

Your alarm goes off. You hit the snooze button. *Just a few more moments of peace.* Then it goes off again. *Damn. Get moving. There is not enough time.* You put one foot out of bed. To-do lists crash into your brain: tasks, appointments, groceries, emails—oh, those emails!!—bills, meetings, and dirty laundry. *Can it be Thursday already? Hurry, you'll be late!* You find your keys and go. Grabbing coffee, you think about all you have to do.

You are now living in a place we call Zombieland. Sure, it is a silly name, but it is easy to remember.

The traffic is taking so long. Why are there so many bad drivers? Hurry!!

Finally, the caffeine kicks in.

Throughout the workday, your mind wanders, dreaming of a vacation. Today is a zombie day. *Please let the day end,* you think. *I need to get more sleep.*

Zombieland days are filled with this kind of dullness, one task following another. Challenge after challenge. You often wonder how you'll manage. So, you try to sprint through, rushing tasks, burning through time, ending each day exhausted. Perhaps you fall asleep wondering, *I've spent weeks, months, years living like this. What do I have to show for it?*

Ask yourself, how many days do you live in Zombieland?

One out of seven?

Four out of seven?

None of them?

All of them?

Is life all struggle with no choice? Where is the exit from Zombieland?

Occasionally you stop, and when you do, you realize those to-do lists have stolen your life. And maybe, in those moments, you'll also wonder how you let your life get so busy, task-focused, or boring. You might even slip into thoughts like, *What's the point?* And then, you might slip into blame—why did you let this happen to your one precious life?

In Zombieland, the day's duties deplete your heart's core.

Pause and notice just how this place feels for you.

Have you had enough?

ARE YOU LIVING LIKE A ZOMBIE, OR BUILDING YOUR VITAL LIFE?

Day Two

Let's experience a different day. Imagine the following happens.

You wake up, stretch, and look out at the sun rising over the horizon; the light spreads across the sky and into your room, warming you. You have so many deadlines, but on this day, you pause and appreciate the sun rising. *I will be in my life today*, you say. Today, you choose to live with all your heart, no matter how busy you are.

This is a new world we call Vitalityland (yep, just another silly name). In Vitalityland, the residents live each day as if it matters.

Pausing, breathing in morning air, you ask yourself, *What matters to me today? What do I care about?*

And then you listen.

You decide to direct your energy with awareness into your valuer, keeping values and longings close.

You enter this busy day in Vitalityland asking yourself, *How can I create vitality?* And you answer with action. Maybe that is brushing your teeth and watching birds in a tree out of your bathroom window, deciding to let the to-do lists go for a moment. Perhaps you smile at the person making your coffee or share a joke about the weather, noticing the softness of their deep brown eyes. As you go about the day, you remind yourself of what's important, and in doing so you create more energy. Maybe you pause to ask a coworker how things are going. Maybe you stop to take a relaxing lunch.

You direct your energy toward vital moments, *and* still work hard.

You phone a friend and share an internet meme with a laugh, put the phone away to look at your loved one speaking, take a moment to yourself, *and* still, you get tasks done.

As this day ends, you pause, sitting on the edge of your bed. You smile and notice it was the smallest of things that made today worthwhile. You're still tired after a hard day's work, but there is a warmth in your heart. Today you stepped into vitality with small actions that brought energy.

Pause again, and notice what it would be like to live every day like this.

These Two Days Will Change Your Life

Ask yourself what happened as you imagined Zombieland. Can you describe it in a couple of words? Perhaps you felt low, or dread, or lifeless, or stress rising. And then, ask yourself what happened as you imagined Vitalityland. Describe what that felt like. Perhaps slowing down, or feeling connected, or energized, or vital. And maybe you also felt loss, sadness, and regret. It's unique to you, and anything you realized is fine. You cannot be wrong here.

Are you ready for the big reveal?

If you could experience Zombieland and Vitalityland as *different*, then you *changed*. And get this, *you changed just by reading some words printed on a page*. Even if it was only a teeny bit, *you still changed*, and yet nothing in your physical world changed around you. You were reading this book. You didn't get a better job or a new life. Not a single thing outside of yourself changed. This point matters because it is the first key to releasing you from pointless struggle and creating change. Change comes from within.

> What makes your life feel stuck, as if you're a resident of Zombieland? Is it trying to please everybody and do everything, fear of uncertainty, trying to avoid failure, not knowing how to change, or something else?

Value Affirmation Harnesses Vital Energy

Science shows you can change your life by first thinking about what you value.[2] That was our motivation behind the Zombieland and Vitalityland exercise, to kick-start your thinking.

Value affirmation—speaking or writing about what matters—leads to valued action. For example, when researchers asked students to write about values, students improved their grades and GPA averages, and they even took more classes, whereas goal setting alone did not help them.[3] In another randomized double-blind study, African American students from lower- to middle-income families wrote about their personal values, and their grades improved by an average of 30 percent.[4] It goes even deeper; research shows that if people hold their values in mind, they can withstand pain longer,[5] and persist with challenging tasks.[6] Doesn't valued energy sound like something you need? It's a way to improve your performance, achieve your goals, manage your challenges, and develop the life you really want.

You've started the first step already, thinking about what matters to you—today. Of course, there'll be challenges, and it'll get hard, but for now, see whether you can stay with us. We promise by the time you have read the first four chapters in this book change will seem a lot easier. For now, know this: step one means understanding your human superpower—that's your mind—

and how you can change your world by putting your energy into affirming what you value. When you face uncertainty or unwanted change, become a valuer. Write about what you long for. Let yourself dream.

....
Find Your Value

Facing change begins by first tuning in to vitality in each day, as we did above. And then, as you progress, you will learn how to use small pivotal moments to create valued action. You can use your values and vitality to generate a sense of purpose in your life. You'll build awareness of what matters in your heart and use that to get out of bed, face tough challenges, and keep moving with purpose.

Stepping toward values has changed our lives and the lives of the people we serve. It'll change yours too. Here is an example from Louise that can show how values can change us.

> I was living in Kathmandu, Nepal, when a series of earthquakes struck. The experience was terrifying, but the aftereffects have been life changing and continue to fire me with valued purpose.
>
> Valued action happened on one hot monsoon day, a few weeks after the quake. I sat in the tiny one-room apartment. Overwhelmed. Heavy with despair. A small part of me wanted to leave the country, to escape. But my Nepali family couldn't run to a safer country like I could. I saw them working hard to pull down rubble and rebuild.
>
> "Do more," I ruminated. "You didn't almost die for nothing."
>
> I wished I was a nurse or a builder, something more practical. My clumsy Nepali speech left me frustratingly useless.
>
> My heart was heavy as I thought over and over.
>
> Then a possibility arrived. I teach mindfulness meditation, and my Sherpa partner guides people into the Himalayan mountains. Can these two things combine?
>
> "Let's take professionals to the mountains on mindfulness trips so we can raise money for our local communities," I said to my partner. I had been tired and helpless, yet now I was charged with energy.
>
> I began with one tiny step. Just a simple email to my social network: "Come to the Himalayas with us to help the rebuild. Help us donate to children and villagers. All the proceeds will go to them."
>
> That first step felt like climbing Mount Everest, but it wasn't

technically hard. TYPE EMAIL. PRESS SEND. First steps feel gigantic at the time.

Five people from my network said yes. I knew none of them personally, and yet they were willing to come to the Himalayas. That terrified me. What if they hate it, or get sick or injured? What if, the biggest worry of all, another quake kills us on the trek? On and on went my panic. But my value mattered more than my panic. I wanted to help my Nepali family and I hoped that having some funds raised might help them to rebuild.

One small step led to another. That first trip led to another.

Since then, these trips have created partnerships in impoverished communities, rebuilt schools, helped kids with education, and contributed to health posts. Folks who come with us find purpose for their lives too. And yet, if someone predicted this outcome, I would have thought them foolish.

Even though I felt a lot of fear and doubt, I kept listening to my heart.

That's what your valuer requires from you too.

Listening.

And then beginning by taking small steps.

So, now, we want to turn it over to you. You may not understand what you care about at this point in our book. And that is okay. But we ask you to open your heart and listen to your valuer. Listen to your heart as you read this book. Keep listening and never stop. Do not worry if you don't know what you want. Trust that listening will ignite change.

What do you long for?

If some day in the future you looked back, and your life had been purposeful, if you had lived with all your heart, what kind of person would you be in this one precious life of yours . . .

> » in relationships?
> » in work?
> » in community?
> » in deep care for yourself and others?

Put Energy into Vital Moments and Valued Action

You have now looked at your life through the lens of vitality by asking, *What gives you energy each day?* Then you dove deep into value by asking, *What matters in your heart and what makes life worth it?* Eventually, you'll work out the answers to both for yourself. But then what? You'll have to take action. Valued action can feel risky. Know that this is a normal part of valuing. The more you value or care about something, the more you fear losing it. Let's look at what happens to the three of us when we think about taking a valued action:

Louise: Ouch. "Take action." It hurts just thinking about it. I immediately get negative and predict that I won't take the action.

Joseph: I feel fear. Immediately. I'm afraid if I take valued action in my work, I'll make a huge mistake and might lose everything. I'll end up being alone like I was as a teenager.

Ann: I value being more present, but when I think about taking action on that I am afraid something bad will happen because I am not on guard.

Perhaps you don't want to risk valuing something and being disappointed, making a mistake, or losing control. Maybe you experienced some unwanted change in the past, or have struggled to get your needs met, and you don't want to set yourself up for more disappointment and hurt. But ask yourself, do you want a life that is lived to avoid being hurt? Or do you want your best life? Do you want it even if you might fail sometimes? If you answer, "Yes, I am willing to take a risk to live inside value," then you've taken one step.

> The great thing about your values is they become an energy source that you can always access, no matter how many times you fail to act or act in a way that is inconsistent with the person you want to be.

Let's say that today you didn't act in a way that promotes your health. You can still turn to value in this very moment and choose to value your health. You might say, "My next meal will be healthy." What if today you failed at a challenge—your job interview didn't go so well. That doesn't cancel out your ability to meet challenges. You can always recommit to finding meaningful challenge by saying, "I'll work on my interview skills and apply again." Your values are always available to you, always there to help you recommit.

One of the major barriers to valued action is the sense that you must be motivated and energized to act. This implies that you should wait until you have more energy to start engaging in valued action. There is no need to wait. Your values have enough energy to keep you going. People often view energy as a limited resource, like a battery. The more you do, the more electricity you will use, and the weaker your battery will become. With this way of thinking, the only way to overcome an exhausted state is to rest and recharge your battery. But what if the battery idea is wrong? What if the key to vitality is not doing less activity, but more of the right kind of activity?

Let's shift our metaphor from a battery to a windmill. Wind is endless energy. Valued action creates energy, just like a windmill creates energy from the wind. A windmill does not generate energy by *resting* inside a windless building. It must be out in the world, interacting with it. So must you. The world is filled with energy, just waiting for you to receive it. For example, some people increase their energy when they share a meal with friends, do physical activity, take a walk in nature, build something, play with a child, or create music. It might be worth pausing to think about what actions you do that bring energy, instead of draining you. If you take valued actions like that each day, no matter how small, then you will be fueled with energy.

Will you let your values guide you, and let that energy fill you up?

» If you answered yes, then you've taken your first action step.

» If you answered no, keep reading. We hope you'll find your *yes* in these pages.

Practicing Value and Vitality Each Day

At the end of each chapter, we'll give you a succinct summary of the key steps you can take to begin using your abilities and grow stronger. Here are the steps you can consider for engaging more with your valuer:

Each day, ask yourself:

» How might I use my energy today to create vital moments?

» How can I use my energy today to support what really matters most to me?

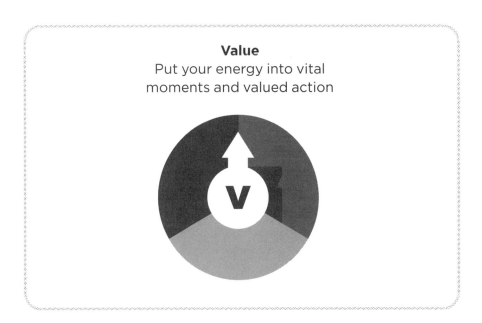

Value
Put your energy into vital
moments and valued action

Chapter 2

ADVISOR:
MAKES YOU
EFFICIENT

Overthinking will burn you out; underthinking
will lead to mistakes; find the middle ground.

We call your inner voice your advisor because it is such a dominant
ability in our lives. And it can be so strong that it can stop you from
discovering new things or noticing your experiences. You become
lost in thought.

Here you'll learn to train your advisor, to use it efficiently, and to let go of
overthinking. Thinking can be a powerful way to change yourself, but also a
powerful way to trap yourself. By thinking, we mean all the ways you use words
to evaluate, problem solve, motivate yourself, and make sense of things.[1] When
unwanted change crashes into your life, you may feel like nothing makes sense.
That's when you turn to thinking. *Why did this happen to me? What did I do
wrong? Can I fix things?*

Thinking is hard to talk about. How do we use words to talk about how to
use words? To make things easier, we use the advisor metaphor. The advisor is
like a little version of you sitting on your shoulder, constantly suggesting what
you should do. Advisors often say helpful things, such as, *You can get through
this*, but also unhelpful things, such as, *You can't handle this.* If you pause now

and just stop reading, you will hear your advisor. Try that for a few seconds: pause, do nothing but breathe, and listen to whatever dialogue comes and goes inside your head. Okay, now you know what we mean by advisor.

Using the advisor metaphor, we convey two things quickly about thinking. First, your advisor seems to have a life of its own, its own energy and purpose. Have you ever felt like you can't stop thinking about something? That illustrates that you are not completely in control of your advisor, although you've probably tried to be. You can't silence it, force it to say what you want, or kick it out of your head. You can make peace with it, though. Then you can focus your energy on fighting for value, rather than fighting for your advisor to say the *right* things. Second, you carry your advisor in your head wherever you go. This means that even when your advisor says unhelpful things like, *You can't change the way you do things*, you can still change things through your actions. You don't control your advisor, but if you know how it works, you can be a master of it.

DON'T RESIST AND ARGUE WITH YOUR ADVISOR; TRAIN IT AND IT CAN WORK FOR YOU.

Mastering Your Advisor

We will teach you to master your advisor in three steps. First, you'll learn how to see it and get to know it. Second, you'll practice redirecting it. And third, you'll learn how to rule it. Practice all three steps and you have an ally that will help you grow through change, rather than being an enemy of change

Step 1: See It

You are going to spend the rest of your life with your advisor. Imagine that. Your inner voice will be there, talking to you your whole life. Consider it this way, if you had a person moving into your house for life, you'd get to know that person, right? So, let's get to know your advisor and how it came into your life. The more you understand your advisor, the more effectively you'll use it when you face uncertainty.

When you were a one-year-old child, you had no advisor. That is, you didn't have language yet. You understood the world through your senses. Words like *mom*, *dad*, *sun*, and *grass* were just meaningless sounds. They could have been any sounds, like *smorf*, *blorbgeek*, and *nidlescrunge*. If you saw the sun, you wouldn't have labeled it *sun*, but merely observed it as an orange ball that felt warm. At this wondrous age, you were living without your advisor, and it was a time of pure awareness. This time would not last long.

As you grew, people around you kept saying words like *mom*, *dad*, *sun*, and *grass*. Soon you learned to make words too. And then you learned to make evaluations: *The grass is a nice green. Grass is itchy.* Then came predictions: *I will be unhappy if the grass makes me itchy.* Then, as the importance of social connection increased in mid-childhood, you developed comparisons: *Am I weaker than him? What if my parents find out I took the chocolate? Are those girls making fun of me?* You can see how you formed your own internal voice, or advisor. Eventually, your self-advice became such a habit that you barely even knew it was there.[2]

And now here you are, with decades of language practice and a constant stream of inner dialogue about yourself, others, and the world. Today, you probably can't even imagine what it'd be like to live without your internal narratives. As a young child, you could sing out of tune and not be self-critical; now, all you seem to do is judge yourself for every slip. You probably never stop to ask: *Is listening to my advisor making my life better or worse?*

It's time to ask that question.

See When Your Advisor Is Helpful

The main reason we all have an advisor is because it helps us avoid making mistakes. It's a tool that has developed over millennia to help us survive. We need to avoid mistakes that can influence our future safety. For example, imagine we give you advice like, "Don't go near that bush, there is a deadly snake there." Now, when you go near the bush, your advisor screams, *Careful*, and you feel fear. Notice how you did not have to be bitten by the snake to learn to avoid it. Our advisor and your advisor saved you.

Here is a workplace example. Imagine that your colleague at work, Bill, spends a lot of time talking to you on Friday night during after-work drinks. You quite like Bill. When he suggests sharing a taxi home, you are tempted. But then you remember a comment your friend Duska made about Bill; she said he made her feel a bit *icky*. Now, remembering these words, your advisor says: *Careful. This is dangerous*. You feel fear about going in the taxi with Bill and decide to put him off. Then, the following week you learn that Bill has been charged with aggravated sexual assault. Your internal voice, your advisor, showed you the way to safety.

> Your advisor makes threat feel present in your mind
> so you avoid risk in the real world.

There is something important to observe here. The advisor made the danger *feel* present. It wasn't just cognitive; it made you feel fear in your body too. You felt afraid of Bill before you had any bad experience with him. This is a fantastic survival skill. The advisor is proactive with its advice giving. It's not politely waiting for you to ask it for advice. It gives advice to you whether you want it or not. That is because its job is to spot threats before you get hurt. It's a sentry. Its primary job is to keep you safe, not make you happy.[3] With regard to Bill, it kept you safe.

> Your advisor is always watching out for problems,
> like an alert sentry.

Perhaps the best part about your advisor is its ability to learn from others, just like your advisor learned from Duska about Bill. Your advisor can also learn from scientists, historians, philosophers, and wise people who lived thousands of years ago. Learning isn't restricted to what you experience firsthand. Your advisor lets you stand on the shoulders of giants, and frees you from having to learn from direct experience every single time.

Your advisor sounds like a fabulous partner, right? How lucky are you!

But . . . (You knew a *but* was coming, right?)

See When Your Advisor Is Unhelpful

To understand the downside of your advisor, you need to understand what makes it uniquely human. Both humans and animals have a biological system that helps them spot threats. Both respond to something slithering in the grass with fear. But unlike animals, humans go one step further. They can respond to threats that are only in their heads.

> Your advisor makes monsters seem present, but what if there are no monsters?

Imagine you have a terrible fight with someone named Samir. As you travel home, you still visualize the fight and seethe with anger. It is as if Samir is sitting right next to you. That is your advisor at work. Then you get home, and your partner has made you a beautiful meal, but you don't see it because your advisor has seated a virtual Samir beside you as you try to work out what you should have said in each moment. As you go to bed, your partner waits for you in a sensual mood, but you have no time for seduction. Instead, you squeeze into bed with your partner on one side and virtual Samir on the other. Tonight, you will argue with the Samir in your head rather than make love.

Animals don't live in their heads or have a verbal advisor.[4] They respond to threats in the moment—when it is physically present. Animals live in the present, but we humans are always fighting mind monsters in our mind worlds. We ruminate about all the mistakes we made in the past, fret about all the mistakes we will make in the future, criticize ourselves for every imperfection we imagine we have, and criticize others for their imagined imperfections. Each of these advisor activities brings new negative emotions and more mind situations. Meanwhile, the tangible world becomes invisible. All humans can become lost in the imaginary world of the advisor.

Being stuck in a mind world wouldn't be so bad if that world comprised unicorns and cotton candy. Unfortunately, for humans, imaginary worlds can be quite negative. It's easy to illustrate this point. Imagine four people say something positive about you and one person says something critical. Will you focus on the positive comments or the criticism? The criticism, right? That is your advisor staying on guard for negative things. If a coworker is friendly to you for four days, then rude on the fifth day, you will likely focus on the rude behavior. Remember, the primary purpose of the advisor is to keep you safe and detect threats, not to make you happy. This means it has a bias toward the negative.[5]

> If you think negatively sometimes, this does not make you a negative person. It makes you normal.

Now that you know a bit about the upsides and downsides of your advisor, you can catch it in action. You'll be ready to watch out for unhelpful thinking patterns. Do any of these patterns sound familiar?

- » *Ruminating about the past.* Do you think over and over about how things used to be? Do you focus on regret and shame, or wish things were different?

- » *Worrying about the future.* Do you think about how changes in your life are going to bring problems in the future? Do you try to make all future dangers disappear?

- » *Criticizing yourself.* Are you caught up in criticizing yourself or trying to figure out what is wrong with you?

- » *Criticizing others.* Are you caught up in criticizing or resenting others? Are you caught up in blaming?

- » *Making excuses.* Do you sometimes make excuses for why you can't do something, such as, *I don't have enough time* or *I don't feel motivated*?

- » *Self-sabotaging.* Do you often have unhelpful thoughts like, *I can't do it, Nobody will ever love me,* or *Life is hopeless*?

Being stuck inside your head and not making any progress on a problem is a sure sign that the advisor is not helping. Maybe it is time to try something else.

» What kind of thinking gets you most stuck right now? Is it related to your work, friends, family, the future, or the past?

» Are you aware when your thinking has become unhelpful? That's when you spend too much time inside your head while life goes on around you.

Step 2: Redirect It, Rather Than Resist It

If you recognize when you're giving yourself unhelpful advice, then it becomes your signal to redirect your advisor. Obviously, you can't kick your advisor out of your head. Perhaps you think you can fight it and try to convince it to be more positive.

What resistance looks like:

Advisor: I'll never find someone who likes me enough to stay with me.

You: No, you'll find someone. Just keep trying.

Advisor: But I've never had a successful relationship. Never.

You: Keep trying. Don't give up.

Advisor: If I keep trying, I might expose myself to more rejection . . .

Does this sound like spinning your brain and getting nowhere? You and your advisor are bouncing back and forth between opposing ideas. You rarely win this fight. Unfortunately, you can't always convince your advisor to say helpful things to you.[6]

So if arguing doesn't work, maybe you could just shut down your advisor somehow? This typically means distracting yourself on social media, binge-watching TV, drinking alcohol, or forcing yourself to think positively and not about the problem. These strategies may make you feel okay in the short run, but they usually backfire and make you feel worse in the long run.[7] Ask yourself whether this is true from your experience. If these strategies didn't backfire, you wouldn't sometimes be stuck overthinking, right? No matter how hard you try to distract yourself, your advisor is still there, inside your head, waiting and watching.

You can't turn your advisor off because it protects you, but you can redirect it. You do this by taking advantage of one simple fact: your advisor isn't your boss. It lives inside your head. You carry it and take it wherever you go, and this means you control your hands, feet, and heart full of purpose. Take action even when your advisor says don't. Listen to your valuer and take action based on what matters.[8]

Stop Trying to Fix Everything with Your Advisor

Think of a time you doubted yourself and did something anyway; that is how you practice being in charge. It shows you were able to have an unhelpful advisor *and* still take effective action. The word *and* in the last sentence is the key to understanding the art of redirection: your unhelpful advisor doesn't need to stop you from doing helpful things in your life. The following sentences provide some illustrations on how to use this practice:

Your Advisor Says	And	You Do What You Care About
I cannot change.	And	You sign up for an online course to learn something new.
I will never find love.	And	You join a group anyway, where you might meet someone you like.
Things will never get better.	And	You do small things to care for yourself and make life better.
I'm too tired to exercise.	And	You use your hands and feet to exercise.
I don't have time to do something important.	And	You set aside time and do it.

> If your advisor is unhelpful, carry your advisor in a new direction.

Here is an example of how redirection worked for Joseph when he faced adversity. As you read, pay attention to his advisor steps. You'll also want to link this example to the ways you get stuck too. At the end of this example, we'll help you think of the steps you can try for your own redirection with the problem you face.

My workplace was downsizing, and I felt under constant threat. My self-talk was loud: "Am I going to lose my job? If I get fired, are people going to see me as weak? Will I ever get a good job again?"

Upper management reframed my research work as irrelevant and an unnecessary expense. My colleagues knew I was a target for firing, so my advisor began to focus on them as if they were the threat. I'd say to myself: "Does everybody think they are better than me? Are they judging me?" The more I thought like this, the more stuck I became. I didn't turn to anyone for help; I just thought a lot.

My advisor worked and worked. It questioned: "What do I have to do to get people's respect? What if I lose my job today?" It blamed: "People have no right to look down on me. What do they know anyway? Screw them." It predicted the future: "I'm in danger. I have to escape now, or they'll destroy my soul."

I got nowhere and generated more and more stress and sleepless nights. After months of investing my energy in my advisor, all I had to show for myself was resentment and stomach-wrenching pain. Thanks, advisor! My life got heavier. Something had to change. Eventually, I saw what I was doing and began to redirect my energy.

....

Redirection 1. My advisor said, "Nothing will help," but I didn't let that dominate me. I had negative thoughts *and* I decided to try something anyway. I confided in my colleagues; I thought that might help. I found out they felt as powerless as me, so nothing changed outside, but at least I knew I wasn't alone anymore.

My advisor said: "Nothing will help," *and* I tried something new.
My advisor learned: Other people were in a similar situation to me.

....

Redirection 2. My advisor was also telling me that people were judging me. I suspected that I had started to see threats everywhere, and I should test whether they were true or false images of people. So, I did the opposite of what I felt like doing. My advisor said, "Don't trust people," and I slowed down and positively engaged with people anyway. I started talking to them about things unrelated to work: "Hello, how are you feeling today? Oh, wow, your daughter scored two goals. That's awesome." Once I chose redirection, my vitality started returning. My advisor no longer held me in its grip.

My advisor said: "Don't trust people," *and* I engaged with people anyway.
My advisor learned: My colleagues weren't constantly judging or disliking me.

Redirection 3. I wanted to increase my self-care activities in response to stress, but my advisor said, "You don't have time for that. You are going to lose your job if you get behind at work." Still, I knew I had to manage my stress or I would burn out. So once again, I tested my advice. I carried my advisor as it repeated negative thoughts *and* I increased the amount I exercised, read, and listened to music. To my surprise, I discovered that doing these extra things did not cost me time at work. If anything, I had more energy for work.

My advisor said: "You don't have time for exercise," *and* I exercised anyway.
My advisor learned: Exercise gave me more energy at work.

Redirection is about training your mind to work for you. You train your advisor by gathering new experiences.

Practice one redirection now	
Choose one specific statement you're stuck on. Stuck thinking sounds like, *I have no time. I can't change. I'm not good enough.*	*Example:* My actions are too small to make a difference to sustainable living.
Redirect it with "and." Take the stuck statement and add a new action.	*Example:* My actions are too small to make a difference to sustainable living, *and* I'll look for ways to influence my community groups.
It's okay if you don't sense change as you read. Change is a lived experience; it happens when you carry your advisor in a new way and try the redirection. Give yourself a chance to learn through practice.	

Step 3: Rule It

The first two steps lead naturally to step 3. If you can see when your advisor is unhelpful and redirect it, you will develop and change. This final step is to put your learning into new *rules of thumb*. We say *rules of thumb* because rules should be flexible rather than rigid commandments. Advisors tend to create self-rules that are inflexible. You'll hear closed phrasing like *can't* or *have to*. Joseph's was: *I can't get past this*. You retrain your advisor by creating new rules that open up, that have phrasing with a bit of possibility, like *might* or *perhaps*. Joseph tried: *I might get past this*. (And he did.)

You can think of new rules as self-talk that you use to guide experiences or action steps, or just inspire you and keep you going. Remember, though, when it comes to your advisor, rules always need to be tested to see whether they are helpful. The following examples show what some new advisor rules might be.

Your Advisor Closes Life	You Rule It by Making Open Rules
I *need to* get past all problems to live.	Life has problems; redirecting myself to value action is something I can do right now.
It *won't* work out.	I can trust the process.
I'll *never* get this done.	I can set aside time and start.
I *can't* get motivated.	I'll persist, even when I don't feel motivated.
I *can't* look after myself.	I can care for myself like I would a loved one.
I *have to* be liked.	I can't make everybody like me.

Create one new rule for yourself and see how it works	
Think of a fixed statement you often make as you face difficulty, one that has closed phrasing, with words like *can't, won't, should,* or *have to*.	**Example:** I *can't* change my disorganized work style.
Now, open the rule to one that has some possibility. Use words like *try, maybe, might,* or *perhaps*.	**Example:** I *can try* to practice new organization techniques.

Practicing Efficiency with Your Advisor

Below are the key steps you can take to begin training your advisor for more helpful self-talk. Remember, your advisor is best used to help you build your life in meaningful ways. It's unhelpful when you are just stuck in it, overthinking, or being rigid.

You'll see we've added *advisor* to the key steps image from the previous chapter. You can now practice these two abilities. Give yourself a reminder by posting it on your fridge or taking a photo with your phone.

Value
Put your energy into vital
moments and valued action

Advisor
1. See it
2. Redirect it (don't resist)
3. Rule it (with rules of thumb)

 **Chapter 3**

NOTICER:
STRENGTHENS
YOUR AWARENESS

Wisdom comes from the body as well as the mind.

The previous chapter showed how to use your advisor, and how to recognize when your self-talk is unhelpful, such as when you are overthinking or worrying. Words matter, but your advisor is not your only source of strength. Here we'll show you how to step into your noticer, and how it can match your advisor's power. Here you can embody life, sense it, feel it, and live within it.

Living within a body makes you a sensitive instrument that receives information about the world via the combination of sight, smell, touch, taste, sound, and feeling. You cannot stop or avoid your *noticer* ability. Your five senses allow you to rapidly detect the appearance of opportunity and threat. Bodily feelings provide you with complex information about desirable and undesirable changes in your environment. For example, if you feel fear in your body, you might expect some future danger and take action to prevent that from happening. Anger is a signal that someone has behaved unfairly toward you. Sadness is a signal that something bad has happened and you may need support. Guilt says that you have done something that might be socially unacceptable. Pleasant emotions let you know that your environment is safe and you can explore and socialize.[1]

Can you see how important this embodied information is for adapting to changing circumstances?

If living with our body and senses is essential, why then is it so hard? How can we spend an entire day fighting what we feel or not noticing at all? There is one simple answer: Society teaches us to control, shut down, or suppress our noticer ability.

Modern rationalist cultures have prioritized thinking over feeling—in other words, putting your advisor in charge of everything, including your body. *Mind over matter*. You learn that the feeling of fear should be avoided and so your advisor informs you: *Fear is bad. I can't stand it*. Then you seek to control and eliminate that kind of feeling. With this kind of learning context, you might end up training your advisor to evaluate every challenging sensation as bad. Grief, guilt, anxiety, and sadness all become problematic and need *fixing*.

This leads us to ask an important question: How much control do we have over our feelings? Our science-based answer is—not much control at all. It is not possible for a physiological being to eliminate negative feelings and experience only positive feelings. That makes no sense for the safety-seeking species that we are. The evidence supports this idea. If you are socially anxious, you may avoid social situations because you don't want to feel your heart beating fast and the tension in your stomach. Yet, avoiding social situations only increases the tension eventually.[2] Controlling anxiety leads to more anxiety. If you suffer from depressed moods, you might avoid experiences to protect yourself from feeling failure or rejection. Ironically, avoiding experiences makes things worse. You recover from depression not by avoiding, but by engaging in life while accepting the possibility of failure.[3] If you fear feeling vulnerable, you may avoid letting people get close. But then you cut yourself off from the possibility of connection. Love comes from the courage to feel vulnerable.[4] Notice the paradox? Your attempts to control your feelings give you less control, not more.

> To improve your noticing ability, make peace
> with your body and the feelings it carries.

How long have you spent warring with your body and trying to get the good feelings while shutting off the uncomfortable ones? Are you done with that yet? If you continue to spend more years fighting, is it likely that you will win? Just based on your own experience, you'd have to say no. There are dozens of control strategies: procrastinating, using substances, overeating, undereating, worrying, engaging in self-harm, shopping, using media to distract, suppressing feelings, denying feelings, and opting out of valued activities that bring stress. All these strategies may make you feel better in the short term but not in the long term.

Are you ready to try something different? Are you ready to make peace with your body and stop treating it as an object that needs to be controlled? Your advisor is not in charge of your noticer. They are equal partners. You can experience the world through your body as well as your mind.

In this chapter, you'll learn how to stay with your noticer instead of using your advisor to constantly problem solve. You'll learn how your noticer can expand your awareness and open you up to acceptance. This will make you less reactive and more able to respond effectively in difficult situations. You'll learn to listen to your body as it responds to messages from the world and how the skillful use of your noticer helps you create a life that you want. If you practice using your noticer with the exercises here, you'll learn to let go of the idea that feelings are to be controlled, and you'll gain so much life. You'll also see that you don't need to manage yourself; rather, you need to practice the ability to listen to yourself.

....

How Your Noticer Learned and Changed

Let's explore what we mean by noticing, how it developed as you grew up, and how you've learned noticing through many experiences of hurt, pain, love, and loss.

You, just like all babies, were a noticer from birth. It looked like this: if your body was cold, you cried out in distress; if you felt safe and held, you probably slept soundly; if someone yelled, you'd wail in fear; and if someone made funny faces, you giggled with delight. As an infant, you didn't use your advisor to judge good or bad. You didn't have an advisor yet. Your noticing was an experience unfolding. Feelings and sensations came and went and came again, and you had no control over them. Slowly, though, your noticer ability changed, and you learned not to react immediately to everything you felt and experienced. Responses from others shaped you further, each moment gradually helping you to use your body and senses to take in the world, respond to it, and communicate what you felt to others.

Onward, to your childhood where your noticer changed as dramatically as your growing body. If you grew up in a community of skilled noticers, you had a good chance of learning these three essential abilities:

1. Your body is a messenger.

2. All your feelings are okay.

3. You can choose how you respond to your feelings.

To grow as a skilled noticer means you saw your embodied messages as valuable. It means that growing up as a child, others accepted all your feelings as normal, no matter whether it was sadness, anger, anxiety, or frustration. It means adults framed your heightened emotions as messages that told you something about the world. Adults who were skilled noticers did not punish you for strong feelings, so you were less likely to internalize shame—even for a wild tantrum. They didn't say you were pathetic when afraid or out of control when angry. You learned to label your feelings and practice letting them come and go. Ideally, you witnessed adults managing emotion in themselves and saw them self-correct with compassion—most of the time.

Sadly, most people's childhoods aren't like this. There are multiple points in which your experience may have departed from the ideal. Your culture may have taught you that strong emotions are unacceptable, anger is dangerous, or sadness is intolerable. You may have been told to control your strong emotions and squash them rather than learn how to listen and respond. Adults in your family may have struggled with their feelings, so they couldn't teach you well. Perhaps they were shut off, or lashed out, or were abusive. Maybe they were abused as children and didn't know how to live with their own emotions. And of course, your temperament mattered too; whether you were a reserved child or a gregarious one would change how people responded to you. Finally, your community influenced you, where you may have been bullied, abused, or felt unsafe.

Here are cultural messages that undermine a strong noticer:

» Anxiety is a sign of weakness.

» You should be able to control how you feel.

» You should always feel positive.

» Negative feelings should be hidden.

» If you feel strong emotions, there is something wrong with you.

» You shouldn't worry.

» Feelings interfere with your life.

» You're weird to feel that way.

» And gendered messages—don't cry, man up, don't be a girl, don't be so emotional.

With all this teaching, you may think change is impossible. Do not despair. It's never too late.

If you've relied on emotional control, this does not make you broken. It makes you a normal human being who has been taught to war with yourself.

You can make peace with yourself.

Changing your ways isn't easy, but you can change if you are willing to use your noticer differently. Remember that you can grow stronger even if you carry a difficult past. Here's Ann's example of noticing and how she changed from being in pain and closed off from her body to being open and embracing life.

When I was young, I learned danger was everywhere—dangerous people, risky places. "Be careful!" was my mantra. I went to a tough school that confirmed this. Social survival came first. And with each passing year, my anxiety grew.

Adults around me reacted to my anxiety by telling me to control it. "Stop worrying," they said. "Just calm down." I understood what they meant; I should know how to control my anxiety. The problem was, I didn't know. It was a mystery to me. So, when I felt anxious, I thought something was wrong with me. It would be years before I realized that my anxiety made *them* anxious, which was something they didn't want to feel, and why they wanted it gone.

My answer to the struggle was to declare war on my anxiety—to prove I could conquer it. I pushed myself into things that made me scared. I pursued the high-pressure career of acting; I liked the challenge it presented. If I could do something even though I was frightened, I'd conquer anxiety, right? Then I'd be safe and could live more easily. I expected my anxiety would disappear once I faced such fears. But it didn't. This is where I stood with my noticer:

Did I recognize that all feelings are okay? No, I thought anxiety was an enemy and made me weak.

Did I treat my body as a valuable messenger? No, I treated my body and the anxiety it held as something I needed to control, dominate, or ignore.

Did I choose how to respond? No, I was reacting to my fear by doing something I did not value.

Survival became my way of life. Until it unraveled me. I felt tired but could not rest because I had too much to prove. Then, I got sick, occasionally at first, then every other week. Soon, I was well one week and bedridden the next, a cycle of exhaustion. Fear and stress were making me sick. Even so, I denied my symptoms and refused to listen to my body telling me there was something wrong. Instead of resting to recover, I would lie awake terrified, churning over upcoming performances and assignments. *I will fail. People will think I am weak. They won't want to know me*, I told myself.

And still I continued.

I denied my fear, got sick, and extended my deadlines. I was disconnected from my body and sense of meaning. Yet I pushed harder. I didn't want to be the weak, vulnerable, and helpless version of myself I despised.

Eventually, I ran out of fight. I needed to stop. I needed to rest. My body was in charge. It was forcing me to listen.

I began to tune in. *Slow down—turn off the light and sleep*, my body told me. I listened more. I began noticing what I needed. I didn't enjoy my life or value most of the things that were dominating my time, like trying to make it on the stage in the theatrical world. I began to realize I didn't care whether strangers approved of me. Instead, I started noticing I enjoyed small moments that no one would ever see or admire. Like talking to my mom about everyday stuff, watching my pet rooster scare away the dog, and working with my mom in the garden, feeling the sun and warm earth. These moments mattered. I valued all these moments more than controlling my fear. Slowly, my vitality returned.

» Are you able to listen in to your noticer and hear what your body needs?

» Are you ready to let go of your fight with your feelings, and instead fight for what you really want?

Strengthening Your Noticer

Ann's experience was long and painful, but it led to growth. It's possible for you to grow too, always. You can strengthen your noticer, no matter what your history. Now we'll turn to teaching you how to develop your noticer with two action steps. You'll learn how to notice-inside and notice-outside.

Noticing-Inside

Noticing-inside is a step to change how you respond to your inner world, a step toward living acceptance on a moment-by-moment basis. Research shows that it's common to develop noticer actions that don't help, such as controlling feelings or shutting off.[5] Ann showed how awareness of her inner experience helped her rebalance herself in a way that led to value. The research says it can work for you too. [6]

If you were to write an account like Ann, showing ways in which you've ended up stuck because of failed control strategies, what would you say? Do any of these control strategies sound familiar?

- » Distract with media, internet, TV, or other strategies.
- » Block it out with alcohol, drugs, or medications.
- » Avoid doing things that feel uncomfortable.
- » Try to figure everything out so you won't make a mistake.
- » Overthink or ruminate on solutions.
- » Hurt others by lashing out or being irritable or angry.
- » Hurt yourself, perhaps by overeating, oversleeping, or self-harm.
- » Overwork and push yourself harder.
- » Drop out of activities you used to love.

These actions bring short-term relief, but they don't bring long-term happiness, vitality, or valued living. Noticing-inside allows you to be more effective.[7] It involves taking ownership of your inner world and allowing feelings to come and go, just like energy that goes up and down. Are you ready to practice?

Make Peace with All Feelings

Think about an everyday event that made you feel happy, such as time spent with a friend, reading a favorite book, walking the dog, etc.

» Take a breath.

» Make your body into a posture that reflects this happiness. If you found yourself smiling, let the smile rest on your face now.

» Notice all the internal sensations as you reflect on this moment. Notice how your body changes, your face changes, etc.

» Label it—this is happiness. Allow this experience to be inside you.

» Pause and exhale. Wiggle your toes. Release the experience.

Now, think about a recent event where you felt down or defeated, an argument with a loved one, being overworked, unexpected bills.

» Make your body into the posture that reflects that moment of low mood.

» Hold it for a moment, and notice all of the weight inside you.

» Label it—this is sadness.

» Allow this experience to be inside you, just as you did with happiness.

» Now, pause and take a long exhale again, making a whoosh sound as you exhale. Notice the ground under your feet.

That was a noticing-inside practice—it's technically simple but not always easy. You likely wanted to cling to the happy memory and push away the sad one. We all do that. However, when you push away hard experiences, there is a trade-off—you spend so much energy trying to close down your inner experience that you have no energy left for living. If you practice allowing your inner world to flow, like released energy in a storm, you will have more vitality, stronger relationships, and less work stress.[8] Of course, we're living in the real world, and we know that being aware of our inner experiences and allowing emotions to pass is genuinely hard to do. Expect that it'll take practice.

Return, Release, Refresh

Return

Are you here right now? Or are you thinking, ruminating, or problem solving? Just notice wherever you are and say *return*. Return to your breath. Do this for about 10 seconds.

Release

Now release. Let your shoulders drop what they have been carrying. Release your arms and feel the weight drop. Let your face release. Notice any feelings in your body and let them go. With each slow breath, allow your feelings to flow out of you. Release it to the world around you. Let your feelings flow out and across the landscape. Let them go just like the clouds releasing rain.

Refresh

Now become aware of how amazing your noticing ability truly is. Look at all the small things around you right now . . . see a favorite object . . . a bright color . . . a plant . . . the sky. Notice what it is like to embrace the moment. Notice that you can draw pleasant sensations inside you too: the warmth of the sun on your skin, the temperature of the air, the sensation of wiggling your toes or loosening your shoulders. Bring these small kindnesses into your body and let them settle inside you. Be alive to refreshing sensation. Release the experience.

Notice your body's strength. You are able to hold positive and negative emotions as they come and go, able to hold all the energy that flows inside you, as you exhale and inhale.

Let all your noticing-inside just be; let it be.

Noticing-Outside

Noticing-outside is the action step you can use to remind yourself that vitality comes from being connected to the world outside your body. When we cut ourselves off from the world around us, we can get caught in our internal world of fear, rumination, and control. Noticing-outside is the action step you take to shift your awareness and get living. With practice, you will be able to connect with the important moments and people in your life.

Although it is rewarding, noticing-outside can be challenging, because we are so habitually caught up in our minds. Don't turn away, though; practice and you will improve and slowly see the value of this ability.

Here's how it works. Imagine you're having coffee with a friend who is talking about their new boss, and you see their face lighting up with enthusiasm. You are noticing-outside. But then, you think about your old boss who bullied you at work, and you feel agitation rising within. Now all your attention is drawn inside you. You are with the bully, not with your friend. You're barely noticing-outside and you've lost life for a moment to your inner rumination; your attention to the world is minimal. You're thinking of the bully in the past and how you might have acted more assertively. You bounce between the past and self-criticism.

Meanwhile, what happened to your friend and the coffee? You closed off to them. Then you worry that you've not heard your friend's conversation. You've left little space for the outside world.

> » How would your life change if you no longer needed to fight with your inner being?
> » Is there a time when you can practice awareness? Try to think of a specific time when you can practice the Return, Release and Refresh exercise.

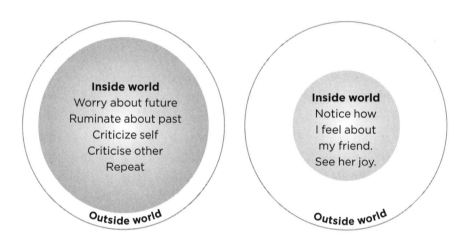

For additional recorded noticer exercises, go to dnav.international

Finding the Moment

When you've lost the world around you, try this exercise.

1. Pause. Exhale.

2. If you're alone, bring all your attention to what you can see and hear outside of you. Come back to the world.

3. If you're with someone, notice the person talking, pay attention to their face and their voice. Be curious, and lean in.

4. Say to yourself, "Be. Here. Now."

Practice noticing-outside but do this gently; there is no need to beat yourself up. Noticing-outside is an ability of returning to life and the present moment. It means you'll spend less time wandering in your mind and more time focused on what you care about. Of course, your attention will always drift, but if you practice returning, you will change, and your reward will be *more life*.

Practicing Noticing Inside and Outside You

Your ability to notice what is happening inside and outside you without controlling it can be life changing. Practice pausing and being aware of the messages. Try it for a few days and see how it changes you. (You can also find additional recorded noticer exercises at http://dnav.international.)

Now you'll start to see how your three abilities can work together. You can step from one to the other whenever the need arises or you feel stuck. You can move to valuer to be more tuned in to what matters. You can step into advisor and problem solve. You can step into your noticer to loosen the grip of your rigid advisor or slow yourself down so you don't overreact to your feelings or the current situation.

Here's the next reminder for these steps.

Value
Put your energy into vital
moments and valued action

Advisor

1. See it
2. Redirect it (don't resist)
3. Rule it (with rules of thumb)

Noticer

1. Noticing inside
2. Noticing outside

Chapter 4

DISCOVERER: BROADENS AND BUILDS THROUGH ACTION

How to have the adventure of a lifetime: Be curious and willing to leave your comfort zone.

W e have arrived at our last, and perhaps, most curious ability: discoverer. Here is a simple example of discoverer behavior, in an everyday situation. A close friend calls you one evening, at the end of a busy workday, just as you're trying to get the last few tasks done. What do you do? Do you usually give them your partial attention, while the other part of your mind is constantly churning on your tasks: *I've still got emails to answer, I must get to bed, I have no time to chat*. Or do you do something you don't usually do? Instead of multitasking, you might try to focus on your friend, listen to their story, and share a laugh. If you gave your friend only partial attention, then you are likely being driven by your advisor; you've got tasks listed and you'll power through them irrespective of all else. However, if you tried something you wouldn't normally do, like making time for your friend, then you have stepped into using your discoverer.

The discoverer describes your ability to become aware of when you are stuck in habitual action or inaction—*I must answer my emails tonight*—or when you can open up to a new opportunity—*I'll enjoy this chat and it'll reinvigorate me*. You might call one place the habit zone, which is safe and familiar. The other is the discoverer zone, where you are curious, explore, and find new ways forward. Sometimes you'll have good, workable habits that you don't need to change, like going to bed a bit earlier if you're stressed. Other times, you'll have habits that only *seem* to work; they make you feel better in the short term but give you more problems in the long term. Drinking a lot of alcohol is a good example; it makes you feel relaxed after a stressful day, but in the long run it is associated with weight gain, depression, and relationship problems. Procrastinating is another habit. It works well in the short term as you sit scrolling through social media, but then you wake up the next day and the work comes crashing in.

Habit Zone
Safe
Familiar
— *is comfortable*

Pause and choose

Discoverer Zone
Trial and error
Curiosity
Exploration
Creative ideas
— *has fear*

This chapter helps you look at your actions and make wise choices. Your discoverer is useful when you face change because it leads to new ways of doing things. Life is always changing—ending or starting relationships, changing jobs, new technology, becoming a parent, children getting older, or becoming a parent to your parents. When change happens, you might continue to engage in habitual actions that may not work anymore. One thing is for sure: new results demand new actions. Use your discoverer to see with new eyes, step into new actions, and learn from mistakes.

Your discoverer creates a valued life through action. The discoverer is especially important when you feel stuck with a problem that just won't budge—like a massive workload. As you step into discovery, you'll also become acquainted with your discoverer's companion—fear of trying new things—but you are no stranger to fear. Step in.

Understanding Discovery Across Your Life Span

As a child, you spent most of your time being a discoverer. You learned about the world around you by seeking and being open to new things—exploring what is under a rock, playing with new kids, and trying things out. A child's uptake of new technology highlights the discovery process dramatically. When a new device comes out, kids will practice it until they master it. They don't have a lot of preconceptions, so they just start pressing those buttons, making mistakes, and learning. But try teaching your grandmother how to use a new smartphone and you're probably in for a long lesson and lots of follow-up questions.

Discovery makes kids better than adults at some things.[1] Children will sometimes try without the same fear of embarrassment. Children are better at detecting unusual relationships in a pattern of evidence.[2] They can also better imagine new uses for tools,[3] remember information that is unrelated to goals, and respond to changes in the environment.[4] The older you get, the more likely you are to rely on your advisor and what you already know, and you'll become reluctant to revise what you think.[5] If this is happening to you, loosen that advisor domination; sprinkle a little discoverer in your life.

It's not your fault that you discover less now. It is fast and efficient to follow your advisor's self-talk. But your discoverer is necessary for creating vitality and value, for getting out of that habit zone and growing. The distinction can be seen clearly when traveling. Your discoverer draws you to experience: *Let's go down that dark alley; there might be interesting shops.* Your advisor says, *Don't go down that dark alley; it might be dangerous.* You see, both advisor and discoverer are essential, but sometimes they disagree. Without realizing it, you might be always giving in to your advisor and settling into habits—wearily dragging yourself to work, repeating the same useless arguments with loved ones, going through the motions and rarely trying new things.

If you stop using your discoverer to grow your mental and physical life, you won't just stay as you are. You'll start declining. Fail to stress your muscles with weight, and they grow weaker and less functional. Fail to stress your mind with challenges and new ideas, and your thinking becomes sluggish and stagnant.[6] You even increase your risk for Alzheimer's.[7]

When you are facing change and have no idea what action to take, it's your discoverer that can help you try different actions until you get through. When you want to grow, it's your discoverer that can lead you to creativity, with new actions to keep growing across your whole life.

Acknowledge Fear, Your Discoverer's Companion

Leaving your habit zone and doing something new or different can broaden your life.[8] Right now, your advisor might be saying that you can't do this, so let's make it clear: discovery actions can be big or small—taking a new cooking class, starting a new business, bringing innovation into the workplace, learning a new skill, shifting careers, or changing a relationship. Ultimately, discovery is about taking a path without being sure where it leads. Maybe your new business idea will fail. Maybe people in your workplace will laugh at your innovation. Perhaps changing your current relationship will be the worst mistake of your life—or not changing it will be the mistake. Change is so unpredictable; it always involves trial and error. No wonder it comes with fear.

Below, Ann shares a dilemma so many parents know, one where change and fear go together. You'll recall she talked about pushing herself to an excessively high standard in chapter 3. Here you'll see how her old fears returned and how she used discovery to change.

> When I had my first child, I wanted to be the best mom I could be. But I also had no intentions of slowing down my career or letting our home life slide. I wanted it all. So, I pushed myself to return to the office early, and in my "free time," I ran full-day training workshops. I'd work all day and then care for my baby, trying to remain present, loving, and patient as I thought "good mothers should be." Often I'd be up at night either breastfeeding or trying to settle my baby to sleep.
>
> I lived in Zombieland, going from one task to another. I was exhausted and burned out. Yet my advisor clung on with its rigid rules and expectations.
>
> Deep change arrived on a morning that started like any other. Just in one small moment of discovery. I was sitting with my daughter outside in the sun. The wind caught her tiny wisp of hair. She felt it, and for the first time in her little life she noticed the sensation of wind in her hair. She giggled and looked around, delighted.

In that moment things became clear. It's strange that it came from such an insignificant event. But it felt significant to me. I realized what I had known for a while—I wanted to be here, with her, all the time. The other stuff just didn't matter anymore.

So I took action, even though I felt fear. I canceled my workshops and informed my boss I would be returning only part time. What mattered to me was being with my child. At a deep level I had known that, but I was too scared to see it. I was on my advisor track. My discovery came through staying open and listening to what mattered.

Although the choice was clear, reducing my work hours filled me with anxiety. I had never done that. I had fear of becoming irrelevant, fear of financial hardship. And this change brought old patterns and fears—I was giving up my career, failing to be a "go-getter." It was almost as if I was giving up parts of me. And yet, I chose to experience fear and be with my daughter.

That is the essence of the discoverer. You need to step into value, acknowledge your fear, and be willing to carry it. That is how you learn and grow.

IS IT TIME TO LEAVE YOUR COMFORT ZONE AND DISCOVER MORE?

Three Steps to Being a Discoverer

The three steps needed for discovery are exploring your yearning, taking bold steps, and learning through feedback. Let's get practical now and show you what you can try. You can change from being stuck to growing in three steps.

Step 1: Explore Yearning

Imagine there is some activity that you might love, but you've never done it before. It is waiting there to be found. What might it be? Building a car, cooking a new cuisine, doing a headstand in yoga, writing a historical novel, learning a new language, attending a meditation retreat? Your yearning might be anything. Here is an example of Joseph exploring a yearning.

> I yearned to challenge myself physically. I love pushing myself to the limit and seeing what my body can do. But how? Should I bike, jog, lift weights, hike, rock climb, swim? I tried all these things, but nothing impassioned me. I couldn't think of what to try.
>
> Fortunately, discovery doesn't rely on thinking. Sometimes it works by trial and error. We stumble into something and say, "Hey, I like this." That happened to me. I wanted my son to learn martial arts so that he wouldn't get bullied at school, so I started taking him to martial arts classes. Soon I was attending classes too, and before long, I discovered I loved it. I discovered martial arts was not about hurting others or being ultra-tough. It was an art form that allowed me to combine speed, balance, and flexibility into dynamic action. It also taught me how to hold fear and anger in my body and stay honorable and calm.
>
> My journey in martial arts has not been easy. I have felt self-conscious at every step. In martial arts class, we are asked to do things like cartwheels, butterfly kicks, rolling on the ground, and swordsmanship. I have had to be willing to feel awkward, uncoordinated, and old in order to learn. Over time, the self-consciousness has faded a bit, and I have learned to accept my body's limitations while also pushing beyond the limitations.
>
> My only regret is that I discovered martial arts at such a late age.

Now, we turn to you. What activity might you love, but don't participate in? Imagine. Dream. Guess if you need to. Your new activity might be playing an instrument, painting, creating an online business, building your social media platform, running a 5K race, wine tasting, or some other activity.

Now imagine you don't try the activity until you are ninety-five years old. Then you try it and discover you love it. You get to enjoy it for a brief time.

As you think about this new challenge, sense how curiosity feels in your body. Does it bring excitement? Or come with fear? Breathe into it and allow yourself to think about the possibility of newness.

> » How different would your life be if you looked for your vital activity now, instead of waiting?
>
> » What do you need to enter the discovery process? Courage? Time? Something else, perhaps?
>
> » Breathe into this and allow yourself to think about the possibility of newness.

Step 2: Take One Bold Step

Now you are ready to use your discoverer to take one bold step. What is your first action into discovery? A phone call? An online inquiry?

Take that one step. That step requires courage. But as William Faulkner put it, "You cannot swim for new horizons until you have the courage to lose sight of the shore." *Ah, but I'm not courageous*, we hear you say.

Wrong.

Courage is not something you possess. Courage is action and it looks like this:

> Take the one step you yearn to take. Say to yourself, *I am willing to hold fear and uncertainty so that I can live better. I am strong enough to carry fear and uncertainty.*

You can become good at being courageous; it can even become a habit. Courage does not involve taking stupid risks or tolerating distress for no good reason. Courage is taking risks to build value in your life. Your bold step begins with a question: *Am I willing to feel distress in order to do something new?*

You answer either, *Yes, I am willing to try something new* or *No, I am not willing*. Nobody can tell you the right answer. Sometimes you will say yes, sometimes no. Both answers are valid. Only you can find the right yes for you.

There are two ways to get to yes. First, you can connect a bold step with a value. Ask yourself, *Is this important to me?* If you can't answer, you might say, *No, I am not willing to work on this right now.* Remember, you don't choose to do difficult things if they have no value. You choose to do difficult things to build a meaningful life.

The second way to get to yes is to choose the size of your bold step. You can choose a small step or a big step. Choosing yes is like stepping off a low diving board or a higher diving board—both are diving in. There is nothing wrong with small steps. For example, if you want to increase your exercise, you might add a five-minute activity to your morning, or even a one-minute activity. That would be like stepping off the low diving board. It goes without saying that if big steps are your thing, go for it.

Lean in to yearning with one bold step

1. If you could increase your health, activity, or fitness, what might you do? Think of a few things.

2. If you dared to learn something new, what would that be?

3. If you could change your actions and work to strengthen a current relationship (friend, family, partner), what might you do? Just take your time and imagine.

4. Now, considering everything, what new action do you want to try? Imagine yourself trying that new thing.

As you think about taking on new challenges, sense how curiosity feels in your body. Does it bring excitement? Does it bring fear?

» Acknowledge any fear by saying it out loud—"This makes me nervous." Then slow your body and breathe.

» Be aware of defensive advisor talk, such as, *I can't do it.* Remind yourself it's normal to have these thoughts.

» Fear is the companion to discovery. Remind yourself that it always passes.

Here is an example of how Joseph chose the size of his step.

Before I discovered martial arts, I was completely sedentary and disconnected from my body. How did this happen? I had once been athletic, but now was badly out of shape. I had to do something. My first thought was to join a gym, but I found the idea anxiety provoking. I had "no time." If I exercised, I would fall behind at work. Also, I felt self-conscious exercising in front of other people. Going to the gym was too big a step.

But I valued being fit, so I chose a smaller step. I started working out for fifteen minutes a day on my back deck, when nobody was looking. It was a tiny step, and many people would think it was a trivial amount of exercise. But through that step, something interesting happened. I realized how much better I felt when I exercised. I was less stressed during the day and less reactive. This is a key feature of discovery. You interact with the world in new ways, and you discover unexpected outcomes. The discoveries aren't always positive; I might have also discovered that I hated lifting weights and then I might have tried something else, like jogging.

After a few months of these fifteen-minute workouts, I got comfortable and realized I was ready for another bold step. I was now willing to exercise for longer. Discovery changed me, and what seemed like a "big time commitment" had become small. I was ready to say yes to going to the gym for an hour. However, I was still self-conscious about my strength. I imagined myself standing in the corner, lifting the lightweight bells, while everybody around me stared. So I made the step easier. I got a membership to a twenty-four-hour gym, so I could exercise early, before anybody got there.

On day one of my membership, I arrived at the gym at 5 a.m., opened the door, and my heart raced. The gym was filled with the strongest and most committed-looking athletes. I thought this was going to be a small step, but now it was huge. This is another aspect of discovery. You can keep choosing to take bold steps, especially when circumstances change. I had to decide: Am I willing to feel this distress, to do this fitness activity? Or should I turn around and pretend that I had opened the wrong door? I chose to walk through the door. That launched another discovery process. I learned that I was virtually invisible in this gym. Nobody stared or cared. My bold steps launched me into a more physically active lifestyle.

Step 3: Stay Open to Feedback

Next is the critical third step. Link your action to value, not just to making yourself feel good in one moment. Your feedback won't always be immediate. You may have to do the activity for a while to discover whether you value it. For example, your first few days learning guitar may be boring, but this does not mean you won't love guitar eventually. Your feedback can also come from others. For example, if you are extending yourself at work, you can seek feedback on your growth, but remember to stay open to negative feedback as well as positive. Often, your feedback will come from within. Perhaps if you start a new workout routine at home or a new hobby like gardening, you'll want to consider whether your activity is building meaning and energy in your life. Do you enjoy it, or is it merely another thing you *have* to do?

All of this takes courage. Feedback is not always obvious. Here is what staying open to feedback looked like for Louise.

The conference coffee break stretched across the hotel lobby. Hundreds of people milled in a crescendo of greetings, hugs, laughter, and excitement. Each year these conference folks gather, and many have become friends.

I watched and felt like an outsider. I saw their connection to each other. Their warmth radiated and made me more anxious. I wanted to be there and I didn't want to be there. Socializing at the conference, or networking in the big hall at lunchtime—it was all hard. I looked around the room, holding my plate. Small groups of people were sitting in huddles or standing chatting. This unstructured part left me feeling vulnerable and uncontained.

I couldn't stand alone. I'd have to either sit with someone or hide.

I am an introvert. I pondered how nice it would be to just be at home, with my garden, my family, and my dog.

I took a breath, walked up to someone, caught their eye, and introduced myself . . .

Now, when I reflect on these experiences, after attending decades of conferences, I know every single one of them starts like this. And each year, I stay open to the feedback from the conference, instead of from my social anxiety. Attending every year gives me a history of feedback. I know that after a day or two, I'll have passed the worst of my nerves. I'll have said hello to lots of people, found my groove, and begun to have fun. I will be glad I stayed.

I also now know that I'm never going to control or eradicate social anxiety, but I'm more comfortable with it. Funny thing about anxiety: I was elected president of that organization, and you'd think that would make social anxiety go away, right? Wrong. It got worse!

And it'll be the same next year; I'll be anxious again. But my values tell me it's worth it.

Looking for feedback from within my heart has changed my life.

Allow discovery into your day, every day, seek feedback, and restart. That is the key to changing your life through action. Discovery brings curiosity, vitality, and meaning into your life because it opens the doorway to valued living. Each day you can try new actions. Don't be afraid to fail. Failure is the pathway to success. Remember that courage and willingness are companions walking with you. Courage is not senseless risk; it's about being brave enough and confident enough in your capabilities to deal with whatever life brings, and it's about taking risks because it leads you into a life lived with value.

> Willingness is choosing your action based not on how it feels, but on where the path leads. Pay honest attention to the outcomes and embrace constant change.

Practicing Getting into Your Discoverer Zone

Now you are ready to practice using all your DNA-V abilities to face changes and challenges. As you go about each day, watch out for times when you are doing the safe, predictable thing, and consider whether stepping into your discoverer zone will be helpful.

We've created this final illustration with all of the DNA-V steps together.

Value
Put your energy into vital
moments and valued action

Discover

1. Explore yearning
2. Take one bold step
3. Stay open to feedback

Advisor

1. See it
2. Redirect it (don't resist)
3. Rule it (with rules of thumb)

Noticer

1. Noticing inside
2. Noticing outside

Part 2

BUILDING STRENGTH WITHIN **YOURSELF**

Self is you, and you are change.

In the previous chapters you used the DNA-V system to respond to change and learn how to transform your life. Now we go deeper. The next five chapters build aspects of yourself—vulnerable, boundless, compassionate, achieving, and profound awareness. You will begin to look at transforming your *self*—who you think you are, how you see yourself, and how all of you can change. DNA-V are the abilities that help you grow your self.

Your self isn't
just a body, young or old,
a heart that beats with emotion,
a breath that renews;
self opens through vulnerability.

Your self isn't
that thing you call *I* and *me*,
not just words like *stupid* or *weak*;
beyond words, you are no thing,
self is boundless.

Your self is
a struggle of past and present blending,
released through an open soul,
the kindness of a friend that lives inside;
self grows through compassion.

Your self has motion,
hoping, trying, failing, and trying some more,
stumbling toward growth,
longing built into a lifetime;
self achieves.

Your self is awareness,
feeling the sun on a warm day,
seeing yourself, sensing your breath,
slowing your heartbeat;
self is profound awareness.

Chapter 5

YOUR VULNERABLE SELF

Respond to vulnerability with stress, and life seems like a constant emergency; shut down, and life is about escape; respond with balance, and life opens up.

Louise shares this story about being vulnerable.

"Put your dishes away," I say.

"Why are you so angry?" my teen demands.

"I'm not angry. I'm just asking you to put your dishes away."

"You are angry; you've been angry for days."

I'm silent.

He continues, "Why can't you just talk about what's bothering you? You never talk about what's bothering you. You just get angry about dishes or something else I'm supposed to do. What's really wrong?"

Is he right? Maybe? My heart races; tension buzzes through me. I feel the urge to argue. I have every right to be upset. But I know where this fight will go, so I stay silent.

One moment I'm washing the dishes, and the next, all my history comes out in an argument at the kitchen sink. Have you noticed that events can escalate quickly? And it's usually with someone close to you, like your partner, child, parent, or someone you care about. Perhaps you're like me, and this argument isn't really about the dishes. It's about feeling stressed and unfairly treated. A struggle like this can be about feeling overworked, tired, and burned out. Or it can be about all those times you've felt misunderstood and your past hurts creep in. Your stress is often held in your body and may make no sense to the rational part of your mind. Vulnerability often brings extreme responses like the need to fight, flee, or withdraw. If you find yourself overreacting, then perhaps the time has arrived to try something new.

In this chapter, we'll show you how you can understand yourself and practice becoming emotionally balanced so that you can face stressful changes, care for yourself, authentically connect, and grow. The first bold step is to recognize that feeling vulnerable is normal. You don't feel that way because you are broken or weak. You don't have to fight the feeling or beat yourself up about it. Humans are hardwired to feel vulnerable and to never forget past trauma or adversity.[1] This is why your past can flood into the present and lead you to feel distressed and confused.[2] Know this: you can experience pain and still live a good life without having to erase your past. Your life will have loss, and you can nurture yourself. Your life will have sadness, and you can keep living. Here we'll help you along that journey.

....

Your Three Responses to Danger

Humans have evolved to survive stressors by using *physiological* and *social* responses. These survival responses are built in and shared with all social mammals. Let's look at an example of one of our close mammal species—the monkey—so that you understand adaptation for survival more clearly. You'll begin to see how your body and brain respond to risk.

Monkeys are hardwired to sense risk and respond much like we do. When monkeys sense threat, their first reaction is to reach out to their kin group for protection. If others come to the rescue, they'll settle down. If others don't help, their bodies will flood with adrenaline and prepare for fighting or fleeing.

Fleeing will usually be the preferred option because it's less taxing on the body than fighting. However, if the danger seems inescapable, they may take the final option and freeze, curl up in a ball, shut down their body, and feign death. This last line of defense might get the attacker to move on to more lively prey.[3] Although crucial for survival, fight, flight, and freeze responses take a toll on a monkey's resources, so a happy monkey thrives if it doesn't need to go into these heightened stress responses too often.

Now, over to you—a human. You were born with the same adaptive responses. In infancy, if you felt unsafe, you could put your arms out, fuss, or cry to get picked up; in other words, you could call on your group for help. If support did not come quickly, you could up the ante by engaging in a stress response—an escalation of crying or fussing. Lastly (and we hope very rarely), in the consistent absence of any soothing, you could withdraw into a complete shutdown, becoming numb and unresponsive. Your physiological and social responses are built from these basic instincts, and then they are shaped by your experiences.

> The body and mind have evolved to detect stress, respond, and survive.

As you age, you acquire more knowledge and sophisticated responses, but these are built on top of the basic responses. They don't replace them. You can now put down a bully with a subtle joke, but your survival side still wants to physically fight or flee. Your body and brain will continue to use your rapid response system. If you see a stranger approaching in a dark alley, your brain and body rapidly dump stress hormones into your blood, your breathing speeds up, your heart rate increases, your hearing becomes sharper, and you physically prepare to fight or flee. All this occurs before your conscious mind can process what is going on. Your social response to danger may be to scream for help, and when you get home, to debrief to friends.

Throughout human history, we see that humans are weak when isolated. Humans are strong when they are in cooperative groups that work together in hunting and defense. You are alive today because other humans helped you, so your social connections will always matter. However, how others helped you also matters. Did your social history prepare you well for life?

The Biological System That Learns

Learning has changed the way your body and mind respond to stressors. As a child, if adults around you were mostly responsive, soothed you, and held you, then you'd have learned to explore the world with a sense that there was a safe base. Over time, you've also observed how family and friends manage their stress or vulnerability. If you saw calmness, openness, and trust, you'd likely imitate that and have a sense of trust in the world and in others.

But what if your experience was not warmth and safety? What if you grew up surrounded by adults who were busy, stressed, overworked, neglectful, or even traumatized? You might have been on the alert and rarely calm or balanced. You'd feel, deep in your body, that no one will help you—you are alone.

Louise shares her story of growing up in such an environment:

I peeked through the crack and watched my drunk father lurching down the hallway, yelling, bouncing off the walls, pulling open the kitchen drawer so that knives fly into the air.

I quickly hid. Pulling my scratchy woolen blanket over my head, I tucked into a ball and tried to disappear. There'd be nothing to see, just blankets.

Looking back, I see domestic violence and intergenerational trauma raged in that kitchen. My father was an alcoholic ravaged by his childhood of neglect and poverty. His lurch down the hall was not just alcohol but also his deformed leg, a remnant of childhood polio. As a teen, he lashed out in anger at the world. He was sent to a boys' "reform" school that was cruel and harsh. His escape on a cold winter's night flashed into the newspapers—a teenage boy huddled in a sheep paddock having police fire shots at him. During World War II, his polio-wasted leg excluded him from duty. He was marked as a coward. His emotional scars ran deep and he fueled them with booze. He lashed out in brutal rage, beating my mother and brothers.

My mother, a woman with six children, fought like a warrior to stop us from being "sent to welfare." That was an ever-present threat I would hear through the house.

I don't know where my mother was when I was small; I have no clear memories of her presence. I do know the violence cost her dearly. She was anxious until the day she passed away, decades later.

My world as a child was threat and neglect. I learned that others could not be trusted. I developed unyielding independence, a common outcome for those with a trauma background but not one that sits well with deep connection and love as an adult.

Back to the present day. I'm on the verge of overreacting to those unwashed dishes.

I know how this goes, a back-and-forth argument going nowhere. I stay silent.

I have a hair trigger for conflict, and that vulnerability puts me on instant alert—the sirens go off. *And*, I don't need to repeat what I did as a child; I don't have to run. It takes a lot of practice. I need to withdraw to restore calmness and then reengage with my values. I practice awareness with my noticer, trying to bring openness and acceptance. I practice meditation. I keep trying. Balance is easier with every practice, and it only takes the smallest of actions; to show vulnerability, to listen instead of defending. My reward is love.

Change is possible. Hold on to that notion. Never forget that you can change.

Your life today isn't just about how your primary caregivers lived. Your temperament also contributes. Plus, your experiences with broader connections like extended family, childcare, teachers, friends, and school. Suppose you were fortunate and had early care that included lots of kindness, love, and good enough modeling? In that case, calm responses are likely available for you to enact in a stressful moment. In contrast, if your early experiences were of heightened stress, then you will have learned those actions too. That's how we overreact to a pile of dirty dishes.

....

Your Body's Balancing Act

Now it's time to gauge how you are doing and what you'd like to change. Your responses to stressors are the outcome of both your biology *and* your learning. Each event across your life, big and small, contributes. If you've been alive for 30 years—that's 10,950 days—imagine how many stressors you've seen and responded to in all those years.

Consider what you have learned to do when you are stressed or vulnerable. You may find that heightened responses come more easily to you than you probably like. Do not despair. Your capacity to change is far greater than you might think. But you will need to remind yourself of one crucial point—learning is only by addition; you can't subtract or erase what you've learned in the past. If you could forget your past completely, then you could also forget where the danger is, and that's not the way survival works. The past chapters of your life are written. You can't change history, but, going forward, you can write new chapters.

> » Your first step to a new chapter is self-awareness. Consider how your whole self—body, emotions, brain, and history—come together to engage with challenge and change.

How do you usually respond to change, uncertainty, or unexpected events?

Stressed	Balanced	Shut Down
1. Your heart races, you feel breathless or edgy. 2. You often experience strong emotions. 3. You can be quick to get angry, argue, or feel a need to defend yourself. 4. You can overthink and ruminate on issues. 5. You become agitated over things that don't seem to bother others. 6. You get agitated in a noisy or rushed environment.	1. You have the energy to address life's challenges. There is room for growth. 2. You care for yourself by being grounded, mindful, or nurturing, or have strategies to soothe yourself. 3. You can problem solve, talk helpfully to yourself, and work your way around a problem. 4. You take action that is curious and playful in life. 5. You connect with others by seeking support and asking for help. 6. You restore calmness and strength by being with others.	1. You feel overwhelmed, ashamed, hopeless, trapped, depressed, or numb. 2. You feel unmotivated and uninterested in doing things. 3. You feel as if you are outside yourself or disconnected. 4. You shut down, go into yourself, and withdraw from others. 5. You are on your guard, expecting betrayal or threat. 6. You are living with abuse, violence, or an unpredictable environment.

Do any of these patterns seem familiar? Let's see what is happening inside your body and brain when you go from balanced to stressed or shut down. First, remember that your nervous system constantly seeks to keep you calm and connected (that's called homeostasis). The parasympathetic system works on this by moving you to get rest and support from others—we've called this *balanced.*

When you feel threatened, your fight, flight, or freeze response (sympathetic system) becomes dominant and your heartbeat accelerates, your muscles tense, your breathing speeds up, and you feel charged—we've called this *stressed.* For example, you see an angry person yelling in a shopping mall; you feel the tension and move away to safety. When you get safely away, your parasympathetic response engages, your heart rate and breathing slow, you feel calm, and resources are shifted away from fleeing to growth and regeneration of the body—you're balanced again.

Shutting down or freezing can happen when you experience intense threat, terror, or have had trauma in your past. Here your body responds with *too much* parasympathetic activity, which makes you numb or frozen.[4] For example, you see an angry person yelling in the shopping mall, you become terrified, and you might freeze, or have bodily reactions of numbness and even dissociation. Shutting down can also take the form of depression and inactivity.

Neither the sympathetic nor the parasympathetic system ever *wins* this competition. Your heart rate constantly fluctuates, sometimes beating faster as the sympathetic system activates and then slower as the parasympathetic system activates.[5] To use a car metaphor, stressed is excessive use of the gas pedal, shut down is excessive use of the brakes, and balanced is using both pedals effectively to drive toward what you value.

Balance comes when both the parasympathetic and the sympathetic systems are responsive to environmental change. This is reflected in a heart rate that is not static but is always varying, always ready for any situation. Research confirms the value of a changing heart rate. Higher heart rate variability is associated with less stress, better self-control, making wiser choices, and a lower likelihood of dying.[6]

Remember, your response is not about logic and what your mind believes. It is about what your body and brain sense. You sense danger—its job is to rapidly detect risk, respond, and get you back to safety.[7] Feeling stressed or shut down is not bad or wrong. It's when you have *constant* stress, overreaction, or overwhelming feelings that you'll want to work toward change.

NOTICE WHEN YOU ARE OUT OF BALANCE AND PRACTICE TAKING YOUR BODY HOME.

Practicing Balance

Now you are ready to learn the two steps to achieving balance.

Step 1: Evaluate Your Responses

First, evaluate how you are doing.

> *Stressed:* Consider the six items in the stressed section of the stressed–balanced–shut down chart you saw earlier in the chapter; how many would you say yes to? If you agreed with most items, it's a sign you're stressed and need some rebalancing practice. Your advisor likely charges up trying to resolve problems by overthinking. Your noticer registers strong reactions—anxious, panicked, angry, frustrated, or irritable. Your discoverer uses habitual responses, like overworking, lashing out, yelling, slamming doors, or avoiding the situation and hiding away. All these stressed actions take a lot of energy and can leave you spent. You won't have much energy for value and vitality. If you spend too much time stressed, it's difficult to get stronger because you focus so much energy on surviving rather than living your life. This is not a reason to beat yourself up. We all have work to do to get better.

> *Balanced:* If you mostly chose these items, then good for you. You've probably worked hard to maintain your equilibrium. Keep doing what you are doing!

Shut down: Out of these six items, how many describe you on most days? If you agree with just a few, you can move to step 2 and practice awareness and balance. However, if you agreed with most items, you might be in a difficult place now and perhaps have suffered trauma in your past. Studies show that some form of trauma is experienced by around 70 percent of the population.[8] Sometimes it's a one-off event like a car accident that we can recover from over time. However, sometimes it's abuse, neglect, or trauma that can be hard to integrate into your present life without help. Shutting down *often* is a sign that you might consider seeking help from a professional of some kind. Emotional distress is not your fault, and it isn't an internal weakness. You are not to blame.

Step 2: Restore Balance

Regardless of which responses you are using, you can help yourself by practicing actions to restore balance. *Balance* is often a popular catchword for health and well-being. However, when we talk about balance, we focus on a science-based concept of change that can occur at the level of your physiology. On the surface, balance simply means caring for yourself and connecting with others. At a deeper level, balance involves activating your parasympathetic nervous system, and increasing your sense of calm and psychological strength. You will also be able to activate your sympathetic system if needed, say if there is an imminent stressor, and then deactivate it once it has passed.

When you are balanced, you'll improve immune functioning.[9] You increase your ability to be with others and enjoy it. You may even get a bonus release of oxytocin, a hormone that increases your ability to relate to and connect with others. Balanced responses are growth responses that build your sense of vitality and value.

Practicing these abilities of balance will help you grow.

Boost your balance with the basic noticer practices—noticing-inside you noticing-outside you (chapter 3). Practice becoming aware of when you're tipping into stress or shutting down. Pause, slowly exhale, name how you are feeling (e.g., *I'm upset now*). Then ground yourself by noticing-inside you—feeling your feet on the floor, wriggling your toes, slowing your exhale. If you're stressed, noticing-outside you can be powerful. Do this by slowing down and bringing your full awareness to what you can see, hear, touch, taste, and smell. Practice connecting with things that soothe you, like your pets, music, yoga, baths, walks outside, a cup of tea, exercise, etc. There is no limit; it's about knowing what works for you.

Reaching Out for Help and Connection

In times of stress, we long to connect to and be heard by others. Connection is a crucial aspect for us as a species. If you're stressed, try to first reach out to people you care about and ask for their help. With people you trust, show your vulnerability and remind yourself that it isn't weak to need others—it's human.

Make it a two-way street by caring for others too; research shows that giving to others is associated with higher happiness[10] and better mental health.[11]

Pause, Reset, Plan

If a stressful event is happening right now, practice this Pause, Reset, Plan routine:

1. **Pause.** Stop doing everything. Breathe out long and slow. Notice your breath as you do this. Try not to change your inhale; just slow your exhale.

2. **Reset.** If you can, allow your gaze to reach off far into the distance for a few seconds; see the sky if you can.

3. **Plan.** Remind yourself of your values or vitality. Right now, I want to . . . _____.

To create further balance in mind and body, take action with lifestyle and environmental changes. Sleep, diet, and exercise come first. These three are essential to maintain your balance. Studies show sleep, diet, and exercise reduces stress, increases biological balance, keeps your weight down, creates a greater sense of well-being, and helps you live longer.[12] It makes sense if you think of yourself as an ecosystem that you need to care for.

> Your body is a sensitive instrument. Care for it with physical activity, sleep, and healthy food, and it will accurately guide you toward meaning and joy.

Discover new ways to resolve stress. Engage in curious and compassionate problem solving with yourself and others. When it comes to your advisor, watch out for those stuck thoughts. If your self-talk is very loud, step into your noticer and use practices to calm your body first. Then practice getting flexible with that self-talk. Finally, treat yourself with more compassion (see chapter 7). Give yourself quiet time when you need it. Do kind things for yourself. Remind yourself that you are a complete person, you are not broken, and you can restore yourself to calm.

Practicing to Rebalance Your Embodied Self

We've summed up the steps you can take away from this chapter in our balance beam illustration. Throughout the day, connect with yourself, notice what is happening, and then take small steps to rebalance yourself. Try putting this somewhere as a reminder.

Evaluate and rebalance your embodied self

Reach out for help and connection

Practice slowing breath, grounding, mindfulness

Use helpful advisor talk, sleep, and exercise routines

Stressing: Racing heart, breathless, edgy, strong emotions, quick responses, defended, overthinking, agitated, pressured

Shutting down: Overwhelmed, ashamed, hopeless, trapped, depressed, numb, unmotivated, disconnected from self, withdrawn from others, on alert for threat

Chapter 6

YOUR BOUNDLESS SELF

Your thoughts cannot capture all of you. You are not words. You are boundless.

Society and other people often teach you that you are limited. Don't assume they're right. The evidence shows that limitations are often self-imposed, not real. For example, you probably learned that intelligence is inherited, so you can't improve it, but now there is clear evidence that it can be improved.[1] I (Joseph) am an example of this. I went from being in remedial classes and classified as stupid in high school to getting a college education. If I had believed others, I wouldn't have tried to educate myself. Here's another false idea: you learned that genes are destiny. You can't change them. Yet there is now clear evidence that we switch our genes on and off.[2] Finally, you were taught to doubt yourself and set *realistic* limits. "Who are you to dream big?" people ask. Yet research shows that if you have hope and dream big, you can often achieve much more than your doubting mind thought possible.[3]

This chapter is about breaking free from your self-imposed limitations. Awareness of your labels is your first step toward freedom. What labels do you slap on yourself that might be limiting you? Do you use labels like *strong, weak, masculine, feminine, lazy, extroverted, old, young, creative, neurotic, broken?* You probably have quite a few. We'll show you that it doesn't matter how many, nor does it matter whether they are affirming or critical. Become aware of labels, and they start to lose their power.

Ask yourself, do your labels prompt you to grow and change? Labeling often becomes a trap, preventing you from moving forward in your life and growing.[4] For example, imagine you 100 percent believe *I'm too old*. How will you act when you tell yourself this? You'll deny yourself things you classify as *only* for young people. That could include learning a new language, studying, taking up a new hobby, playing a sport, or anything. You now act *older* simply by describing yourself as too old. Before you know it, you'll be clicking social media links for walking canes instead of walking tours. Lots of labels can trap you like this, for example, *not good enough, broken, not smart enough, unlovable,* and *powerless*.

To grow and change, you need to become aware of your labeling traps and escape from them. This idea can be understood metaphorically. There was once a cruel practice for trapping monkeys: the trappers would put a banana inside a heavy jar with a narrow opening. The monkey could reach in and grab the banana but it couldn't pull the banana back out through the narrow opening; its hand was stuck in the jar. All the monkey had to do to escape was let go of the banana, but it wouldn't let go. The same thing can happen with humans: our advisor grabs a label and won't let go. That's when you know your advisor is not helpful.

> » What kind of person are you?
> *Are your answers labels that define you?*
>
> » What are you good and bad at?
> *What labels or descriptions do you get stuck with?*

Here is a story that illustrates how Joseph was trapped and eventually got free.

As a teen, I struggled to get my dad's respect. He'd divorced my mom when I was small and was forced to take care of me when she deserted us. He deeply resented this—and me. He was harsh and critical; kindness was rare.

He often attacked my intelligence by trying to convince me that I was stupid. I became scared of being stupid so much that my life became defined by the label "stupid."

I didn't want "I'm stupid" to be true. I didn't know the DNA-V system back then, of course, so I didn't know how to let go of the label.

Instead, I battled against being stupid, a battle that was ultimately valueless. I argued endlessly with my dad about intellectual things. I tried to prove I was smart by fighting his advisor with mine. It never worked. I used my noticer to be on alert for signals of my dad's moods. I'd try to avoid him when he was in a bad mood because it was a risky time where he'd try to make me feel confused and stupid. I used my discoverer actions to get in trouble at school because I wanted to defy my dad and all those adults who thought I was stupid.

In the end, I obtained a college degree and then a PhD. Notably, both are in psychology, the same field as my dad. All the way, I was battling "stupid." I had to get a higher degree than him, just to prove to myself he was wrong.

Gradually, I became aware that much of my life was lived to avoid six letters:

STUPID

I often wonder how many years I wasted trying to escape these words.

About ten years ago, I finally stopped trying to fight stupid and started putting my energy into things I love. I started learning how to play piano, developing a better jump shot in basketball, expanding my physical skills in martial arts, and working with disadvantaged youth. I started all these activities late in life. Had I not been so busy trying not to be "stupid," I wonder whether I could have used my DNA-V abilities to become a pianist or work in physical fitness. Who knows? The past is gone, the present is here. I hold on to one idea now—there is still time for a bigger life.

If you can become aware of your label trap, you'll see that freedom comes from letting labels go. Sure, it takes practice because our advisor is like that monkey. With practice, you can move beyond labels and be boundless, ready for growth and transformation.

Who Are You Really, Labels Aside?

Joseph: *I am not stupid, and I'm not smart either.*

What was that I said?

Stupid and *smart* are words. They are not *me*. Stupid and smart are tools I can use, when they help me, and put aside when they don't. Sometimes, when playing a sport, I will make a mistake and say, "That was stupid." It motivates me to improve. Other times, I say it to myself and I feel demotivated. That is when I want to set it aside.

I can choose how I use labels. I am not them. Let's see how this works for you.

Repeat each of these *I am* sentences to yourself and remember a time each was true.

You are not a label

I am strong.
I am weak.

I am anxious.
I am calm.

I am happy with other people.
I am happy alone.

I am tough.
I am vulnerable

Did you notice how both the positive and the negative terms sometimes apply to you? Did you also notice there's a contradiction? How can you be strong and weak?

You are not any of these things. Sure, sometimes you might be strong or weak, just as sometimes you want to be social and other times alone. Those labels describe your experience at a moment in time. You can let the moment pass and then experience something else. But, when you apply the label, it can seem like *you are the label*.

WHAT MIGHT YOU ACHIEVE IF YOU LET GO OF YOUR SELF-LIMITING LABELS?

The Observer Perspective: Finding Safe Harbor

We'd like to introduce your observing self, which you can use to free yourself from feeling "bounded" by unhelpful self-concepts. Wherever you are now reading this, see if you can be aware that a part of you can see yourself reading. Can you picture yourself reading? Perhaps you are sitting in a chair a certain way, slumped or upright. See yourself. That's it—you've connected with your observer self. Connect with your observer when you want to get free from labels.[5]

In the previous exercise, as you thought of the labels like strong and weak, there was a part of *you* observing yourself doing this. *You* imagined yourself as strong. Then *you* imagined yourself as weak. The labels came and went, but *you* were still there. You are the observer. You are not the labels. This shows you something important: you are strong enough to hold and observe all your labels. Connecting with your observer reminds you of that.

Can you see how this observer perspective helps you let go of the battle to have the *right* labels? Labels don't define you, so there is no need to fight off the *bad* labels like *lazy*, and cling to the *good* labels like *talented*. Observe those labels, like you might observe a sign on a passing billboard, and they lose their power to bind you.

Here is a quick exercise to connect with your observer self. You will focus on a change we all experience: getting older. You are going to use all your DNA-V abilities to work your way through the aging process.

Practice shifting your view

» Imagine yourself as an elderly adult in the hospital, sitting on a bed about to go in for major surgery. Imagine yourself in that bed now.

» Use your noticer and imagine how you would feel lying in that hospital bed waiting for major surgery. What shows up in your body? Fear? Anxiety? Where do you feel that? Can you see that you are the one observing the feelings? So those feelings don't define you. There is no need to label yourself as anxious.

» What advisor thoughts are showing up for you as you see yourself in a hospital bed? Just see those thoughts. Maybe you're thinking, I am old. I am weak. Or something like that. Just watch what thoughts come.

» Now shift into your discoverer and see what you might be doing as you sit in that hospital bed. Just imagine, for the sake of this exercise, you are being outgoing and talkative. You are making jokes with the nurse. You are talking to loved ones. Observe yourself being outgoing in this moment. This does not make you *outgoing* all the time. That is just a label.

You just shifted from observing your feelings to thoughts to behavior. *You.* Shifted. There is a *you* that observes and is not narrowed by your thoughts, feelings, or behavior.

> You are not just "anxious" or "fearful." *You* hold and observe feelings. Feelings don't define you.

Do you see how you can step into an observer perspective? When you are trapped by self-criticism, stop, step back, and observe yourself thinking, feeling, and acting. Remind yourself that labels or concepts do not define you.

You are the one who shifts between doing, noticing, and advising yourself. Connect with your observer perspective, and you will experience that you are not words. You are boundless.

Watch Out for Positive Labels

You connect with your observer perspective when you want to get free from negative, self-limiting labels. Here is something that might surprise you. You may also want to connect with it to get free of positive labels. You might wonder, what could be wrong with positive labels, such as, *I am lovable* or *I am strong*? Not all positive labels are problematic; it depends on how you use them. Issues arise when you cling to positive labels and they destroy value in your life. Here are two concrete examples of when this happens.

Clinging to the Idea of Being Good

Sometimes you might cling to a label, like *good, talented,* or *brilliant,* or *I'm good at* . . . [fill in the blank]. These labels can become like a precious trophy that you feel you have to keep at all costs.[6] Say, for example, you think, *I am good at my job*. What will happen if you make a mistake? Will you be *bad* at your job now? If you cling to being good, you may avoid feedback on your performance, just in case it's negative. Yet you need critical feedback to improve. You may also surround yourself with people who tell you how awesome you are. You may avoid challenges where you might fail and lose your *I'm good* evaluation. When this happens, you do not grow.

Clinging to the Idea of Self-Importance

Competition can be good when it helps you improve; it's healthy. A problem arises when competition is associated with your self-importance, and you take action exclusively to feel *better than.*[7] You start trying to *feel* good instead of trying to *do* good for yourself or others. For example, sometimes you might buy expensive things hoping to feel like you have higher status than others. Or you might criticize others who don't give you what you want. Or you might disparage those who do better than you so that you don't feel *less than*. The only way you can be *better than* is if someone is *less than*. Note that most of this action happens inside you while the other person can be just going about their life. All this built-up internal resentment puts you at war with your fellow human being.

You need to use your observer to willingly let go of self-importance, especially when it causes angry rumination, resentment, or envy. You are neither important nor unimportant. Sometimes you will be in the limelight and deeply important to someone or something. Sometimes you will need to be in the background, supporting others. Unbind yourself to *importance* and you will flexibly build your own and other people's strength.

How to Use Positive Advice

Only now are you in the correct position to use positive advice because now you know the traps. The observer perspective helps you detach from both positive and negative advice. Then, instead of labels controlling you, you use them like a tool. You can use them to motivate and direct yourself, or you can put them aside, like putting down a hammer when you no longer need to hit a nail.

Here are some examples of how to best use self-advice. If you are engaged in a difficult task, you might say, *Come on, you got this,* rather than, *I have the talent to do this.* The key is to focus on your action, not your label of being good. If you are faced with critical feedback, you might say, *Just slow down, try to learn from this, you can handle it,* rather than reacting to your vulnerability by attacking the person giving you feedback. Use self-advice that will help you feel more effective at handling the task, rather than the emotion attached to the task. Research shows that when positive self-talk is linked to action, it can improve your physical and mental performance.[8]

Consider making your own self-advice that will help you grow and improve. The idea is not to make positive statements to build your sense of self (e.g., I am invincible). Instead, create statements that support your valued action (e.g., I can get better by practicing). Here are a few ideas:

I can change.

I'm doing okay.

I will pause.

I can achieve more than I think.

Slow down, there's no need to go fast.

I've got this.

I trust myself.

I can make space for doubt and move forward.

Practicing to Become Boundless

Your practice steps from this chapter are becoming aware of how your self-talk sticks to you. When you've tipped the scales too far toward positive labels, or too far toward negative labels, practice returning to center. You can also step into your noticer too; pause and breathe, and remind yourself that you are not bound by words.

Becoming boundless

Observe yourself thinking, feeling, and acting; see it all changing.	Use positive and negative advice if it's helpful.	Step to noticer when advice is hurting you.

Negative: Stuck inside self-criticism. Labels define you. *I'm not good enough, so I can't change or improve.*

Positive: Clinging to positive affirmations. *I'm talented. I am liked.* Clinging can stop you from taking a risk/making a mistake/seeking feedback.

Chapter 7

YOUR COMPASSIONATE SELF

Compassion is your path to sustained happiness.

Asha sits across from a study partner in the library, with an open math book on the desk, looking tense and confused. The study partner says in an angry voice, "What are you waiting for? Just focus!" Asha fidgets with a pen. "You're wasting time," the study partner continues. "Come on. You left your job to study, and now you are wasting time. Solve the damn problem!" Asha looks again at the math book and starts chewing the pencil. Exasperated, the study partner yells, "What are you waiting for? Do you want to flunk? Solve it, you dumbass."

If you witnessed this situation, what would you do? Would you tell the study partner that they are abusive? Do you feel anger or shock toward them?

Now reimagine this scenario with Asha studying alone. The study partner isn't there. This time, imagine those criticisms come from Asha's inner critic, their advisor. How do you feel now? Does your anger change to empathy for Asha trying to study? If you can feel compassion for Asha beating up on themselves, it's probably because you beat yourself up too.

When you are having a rough time, your self-talk can be brutal, can't it? What does your harsh advisor say to you? Perhaps, *I'm useless. Nobody gives a shit about me. Life is unfair. Trust nobody. Just give up. What's the use?*

When one person abuses another, like the study example above, it is obvious that abuse doesn't help. The student will become less able to study with all that criticism. If you had somebody criticizing you while you tried to do something hard, you'd be less capable too. Your motivation would slide. Your self-esteem would plummet. You'd likely feel out of balance and tipped into stress or shut down. Maybe you'd even leave the library and find some unhealthy way to soothe yourself with chocolate, alcohol, binge gaming—name your avoidance strategy.

Most of us would show more compassion to a stranger than ourselves. Why don't people treat themselves with the compassion they would show a friend? Perhaps we have never been shown how or known the importance of self-compassion. Here, we'll help you see how common and unmotivating criticism is and how harsh criticism makes you achieve less rather than more. And then we'll look at the practice of self-compassion. You'll see how being kinder to yourself can make you stronger.

Do You Fear Self-Compassion?

Self-compassion is the willingness to respond to your pain and suffering in the same way a good friend might, with warmth, patience, and understanding. That sounds easy, right? But you know it isn't. Self-compassion depends on many factors, including culture, family, and gender. For example, in some collective cultures, self-compassion is seen as a form of wisdom and is salient within everyday life. In contrast, other cultures emphasize individualism and uncompromising independence, viewing self-compassion as a negative attribute.[1] Masculinity and power within a culture might also lead us to devalue self-compassion.

Ultimately, by adulthood, many people fear self-compassion.[2] This fear can be intense, especially if you've been tough on yourself to survive. Your advisor learns to say things like: *Don't let your guard down or you will get hurt* and *You need to be hard on yourself or you will never get everything done.*

Which of the following fear statements resonate with you?

» If I'm kind to myself, I will become a weak person.

» I don't deserve kindness.

» A harsh advisor keeps me from making mistakes or keeps me disciplined.

» The only way I can motivate myself is through self-criticism.

» A harsh advisor helps me keep my guard up and protects me.

If you have been immersed in hyper-tough messages for years, consider how this has affected you.

» Ask yourself: "Am I afraid of compassion?"

As you think about your self-criticisms, do you think they are needed to keep you performing or strong? Not according to the data. For example, speaking harshly to people not only fails to motivate them, but it also demotivates them and reduces their sense of well-being.[3] Young people who speak harshly to themselves tend to experience a reduction in hope and social support over time.[4] Finally, people who lack self-compassion tend to have worse mental health problems, worse response to setbacks, and less motivation to improve.[5] It's a myth to think self-compassion will make you weak.

Here is a simple way to understand how your harsh advisor undermines you. Imagine you are working for an abusive boss who sounds just like your harshest self-talk. Every time you make a small mistake, the boss says things like, "What the hell is wrong with you?" Even when you are doing well, they say, "You're not doing enough. You're going to lose your job if you don't do more." You would probably be afraid. Maybe you would try to please the boss initially, but that would only reinforce their cruelty. They might end up abusing you more: "You've screwed up again. You're useless at this." What would happen to your motivation over time? Odds are, you would become demotivated and less effective at your work. You might even do things to undermine your boss, such as speaking badly about them to coworkers.

You might be starting to see how self-compassion works now. Remember the abusive study partner in the example above? What would happen if that partner started acting like a supportive friend, being encouraging and patient? They might say things like, "It's normal to be stressed about the exam. Try your best. You are doing well." Would you expect the student to do better on their math test? Would you expect them to be happier? The answer is a resounding yes. You can break out of self-abuse by becoming a friend to yourself. Recall how you felt kindly toward Asha earlier; extending compassion to others is helpful to yourself and to others.

....

You Deserve Compassion

Suffering is made worse if we feel alone in it. But here we show that you are not alone in your pain. We do this through an imagining exercise, to first connect with our own suffering and then to connect with the suffering of your fellow humans.

Consider a memory that makes you feel ashamed. Maybe consider something that you'd be embarrassed to share with another person, even though you know you couldn't control the situation. Maybe you were raised in poverty or neglect. Perhaps you got stuck in an abusive relationship, and you feel shame about it. Or perhaps you lost your job in a restructure and struggled to find another one. Or maybe you are mean or impatient with your loved ones, even though you try not to be. Think of any shameful memory that still might make you suffer today. Then, hold this thought while you consider this data on human suffering:

Mental health—25 percent of people struggle with mental health problems in any given year.[6]

Traumatic childhood events—25 percent of youth experience a traumatic event.[7]

Bullying—50 percent of people experience some form of workplace bullying.[8]

Poverty—15 percent of people living in the United States have an income below the poverty line.[9]

Violence against women—35 percent of women in the United States will experience physical or sexual violence in their lifetime.[10]

We hope you see that suffering is common and feel a sense of humanity in this. Can you think of the one in four who has poor mental health among your family, friends, and colleagues? Who might you know that faces gender violence? Do you know which of your friends is the one in two that was bullied? Probably not. We hide our pain. The data show that people keep mental health issues a secret, and many don't even seek help.[11] The Buddha got it right when he asserted that life is suffering; it's confirmed in the data.

You are not alone in your suffering. You deserve compassion from yourself and others. Or let's put it another way: either you deserve compassion, or no one deserves it. Every single human being has made mistakes and suffered. Every human has shameful memories that they keep secret from others.

We discussed why this happens in the earlier chapters, but here is a recap. You can suffer because you get stuck in that habit zone, repeating the same old behaviors instead of stepping into the discoverer zone. You can get stuck because you engage in destructive strategies to control your feelings and because you sometimes allow your unhelpful advisor to rule your life. It's also likely that you forget to engage with your values. It's not your fault; these problems are not specific to you. They are true of all humans.

Here is the big takeaway. Every single human has some shame. Your loved ones will have it. Even super-confident people have it. When you feel shame, you feel inadequate. Shame is an evolutionarily adaptive emotion. It is the emotion that says do better, be better, and keep up with your group. That's why shame is present in everyone. The problem is, most people don't know this and don't understand shame. We feel alone and small. It's the way our feelings and thoughts have been shaped by culture and societal norms. The problem isn't that shame is an emotion. The problem is that we have cultures that do not teach compassion toward failure or struggle, so we internalize our shame. Compassion changes everything because you know your suffering is shared. You know you don't suffer because you are bad, unlucky, or deserve it. You suffer because you are human.

Suffering is not your fault. However, you might fear that if you let yourself off the hook, you won't try anymore, or that you'll mess up or become selfish. That is fear of self-compassion, being harsh on yourself to try and motivate positive action. Let that fear go. Your goal is to grow stronger, not punish yourself. You need and deserve the warmth, patience, and understanding of a friend to sustain your motivation.

> » What would your life be like if you accepted your weaknesses as part of being human?
> » What would your life be like if you didn't have to hide behind a mask?

If you have relied on a harsh critical advisor for most of your life, you won't find self-compassion easy. It'll be a new habit. It will be like suddenly deciding to write with your nondominant hand. With practice, you'll get more comfortable with it.

The first thing to know is that being a friend to yourself does not involve fighting your harsh advisor. Remember, fighting your advisor only makes it stronger. You don't want to fight yourself. You want to *redirect your advisor, not resist it*. The fastest way to do this is to pause, take a step back, and see yourself as if from a distance, like an observer. Remind yourself that you are not your thoughts or feelings; you are boundless, and thoughts and feelings are a changing part of you. Let's do that now.

Practice Friend View

1. Recall a time when you were harsh or critical, that is, when you were using your advisor to beat yourself up. Try to conjure up the words and tone of your self-talk. Here are some samples of what people sometimes tell themselves:

    You are not good enough.

    You are so stupid.

    You're not doing enough.

    Why does everything happen to me?

    I hate myself.

2. Repeat your harsh criticism to yourself. As you do, notice what is going on in your body as your advisor criticizes you. How does it feel to beat yourself up? Where do you feel the tension? Just pause for a moment and experience the self-abuse.

3. Now take a step back. Imagine you are outside your body and standing a few feet away from yourself. You are looking at yourself as you criticize, beat yourself up, or suffer somehow. What does this outsider see? What do you look like when you are hard on yourself? Perhaps you are hunched over a chair or look distracted or sad. Maybe you are rubbing your forehead and looking stressed. Perhaps you are tossing and turning in bed. See yourself suffering the way an observer would see you.

4. Now that you have a clear view of yourself in difficult moments, you are ready to try out friend view. See yourself the way a good friend would see you. Look at yourself with compassion, patience, and warmth. Maybe gently place a hand over your heart and say something reassuring or encouraging. What would your dearest friend say if they saw you struggling?

Don't worry if it is hard to get the *friend view* immediately. Don't turn this exercise into another reason to beat yourself up. Remind yourself that it takes practice. With friend view, you can learn to motivate yourself with patience and supportive words instead of abuse. Become a friend to yourself. This is the secret to developing lasting motivation, the kind you need to transform your life and become stronger.

Create a Self-Compassion Routine

You may feel resistance to practicing self-compassion if it's unfamiliar. You can't use your advisor to convince yourself that self-compassion is a good thing. Your advisor is there to keep you safe, not help you feel good. If you get stuck, step out of your advisor and shift into your discoverer. Experiment with some new compassionate activities and see what happens. If your advisor is correct and your self-compassion leads to trouble, you can always set the action aside and try something else. And, of course, you can always go back to using a harsh advisor. We hope you can experiment and realize it is not for the best.

Practice caring for yourself instead. You'll want to use your valuer here. Choose activities that bring positive energy into your life. Or choose activities that build value over time. We've separated them into two types: activities that nurture you and help you feel calm, content, and relaxed, and activities that challenge you and help you feel excited and enthusiastic. The list is just to get you thinking.

We know from research that people who care for themselves get more done, are more effective, and are happier.[12] Maybe you hesitate because you think you have too much work or household duties. That is your advisor talking. To be a discoverer, you'll need to carry your advisor doubts while you try some new self-care activities. Maybe you will discover that you can cut non-vital activities, like scrolling social media or watching TV. Perhaps you will find that engaging in valued activities makes you more effective in completing your other duties and tasks. The only way to find out is to try something new.

Nurturing Activities Energy = Calm, Content, Relaxed	Fun and Challenging Activities Energy = Excitement, Enthusiasm, Absorption
Be mindful of your breath.	Learn something new.
Get plenty of high-quality sleep.	Exercise (something challenging, like rock climbing or skiing).
Eat something healthy.	Compete in a sport.
Take lunch breaks.	Play a musical instrument.
Go for a walk at lunchtime.	Go on an adventure.
Do something with a pet.	Take on a do-it-yourself project.
Listen to music.	Write a story or an essay.
Connect with friends.	Write software or develop a website.
Get into nature.	Go on a hike.
Turn off your electronic devices.	Solve puzzles.
Exercise (something relaxing, like yoga or tai chi).	Volunteer in your community.
Enjoy a meal or cook.	
Express love.	
Meditate.	
Read.	
Do crafts, such as sewing, knitting, or cross-stitch.	
Do art activities such as painting and drawing.	

» Can you think of any self-care activities you want to start soon?

» Name your chosen vital activity and consider a day and time to do it (it can be just five minutes).

» Start.

Practicing Compassion to Become Stronger

Compassion practices may be unfamiliar to you, so grab a copy of this reminder and stick it up somewhere that you'll walk past each day. When you notice yourself either being too critical or too low in self-reflection, return to balance with these steps. Remind yourself to practice compassion with friend view.

Compassion is the path to sustained happiness

Practice viewing yourself through the eyes of a friend.

Practicing compassion for yourself and others will make you stronger, not weaker.

Discover compassionate routines.

Harsh criticism:
Self-abuse/criticisms bring fear of compassion and demotivation.

Weak self-reflection:
Not evaluating actions, insensitive to self feedback, or feedback from others.

Chapter 8

YOUR ACHIEVING SELF

The key to success is stepping up. Step up
over and over and you will achieve.

t's time to dream big. What would you love to improve or master? Do you want to get better at your career, a sport, a hobby, business, creating, building, programming, leadership, or something else? Just imagine that anything is possible. This chapter is a road map on how to reach your peak potential.

The previous chapters have been preparing you for this moment. In chapter 5, you learned to leave your protective shell behind and let yourself feel vulnerable so that you can grow a bigger life. Chapter 6 showed you that self-limiting labels don't need to stop you from growing. In chapter 7 you learned that you can sustain your motivation through compassionate practices rather than critical self-talk. Now you are ready to grow beyond what you might have thought possible.

The Path of Improvement

If you're ready to improve, this chapter will help. Regardless of what you choose to focus on, your journey of achievement passes through several stages: you'll start at beginner, move to competent, then expert, and finally master.[1] You can choose to stay at the beginner or competent level for activities you don't value investing more time in. However, we don't want to stay at the competent level for things that are deeply important to us. We would like to achieve mastery, but often don't. This isn't because we lack specific genes or talents; it's because becoming a master at something requires slow, steady, and hard work, often over years. And we come up against two big obstacles to achieving mastery:

1.   We have competing demands, like life and other responsibilities.

2.   We let our advisor run our life, focusing on immediate problem solving and not on the things we care about.

3.   We want to avoid the difficult feelings that come with practice.

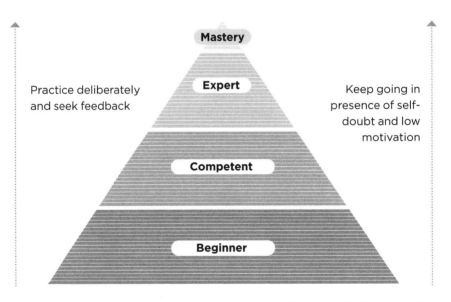

Consider what you want to get better at and how much time and effort you want to put into it. We'll show what each step on the journey might entail.

Beginner is where you have little knowledge or skill. Your advisor might not like you being here. *You look stupid playing that instrument*, it might say. When you listen to your pessimistic advisor, you often don't start the achievement journey. You'll need to redirect your advisor when you make a start. At the beginning level, things will seem difficult and sometimes overwhelming. For example, if learning a new sport, you may struggle to do the essential steps. Everything may seem unnatural or confusing. If learning a new language, you will struggle with every word, and whole sentences may overwhelm your understanding.

Competent means you have some experience and can use your knowledge to focus on what is essential. Things will have become easier, and you might want to settle here: getting good work evaluations, playing your sport or musical instrument at a competent level, cooking pretty good meals, being a decent enough leader or a reasonable programmer, or being able to speak passable Spanish. Maybe this level is enough for most things you do. But is there some passion you want to take further?

Expert level is achieved through many years of hard, deliberate work. Expert means you can perform at your chosen task with ease and skill. The expert guitar player knows instantly where their hands need to go for each chord. The robotics engineer knows how to design new systems. Language experts speak fluently and understand instantly. The expert chef knows which ingredient a dish needs without having to consult a cookbook. Expert performance can seem magical because it appears so effortless. Remember, though, that effortless performance is built upon years of effort.

Master is the highest level in a person's chosen area. They might be concert pianists, business entrepreneurs, renowned authors, CEOs, or professional athletes. Becoming a master often takes a lifetime of devotion.

If you choose, you can travel the path to expertise. Maybe you won't be a professional, but you can become more skillful and increase your sense of accomplishment. Along the way, maybe you'll decide to go to the master level of your chosen activity. Who knows? There is only one path to find out.

1. *Identify what to work on,* which skill you want to develop.

2. *Develop a deliberate practice plan*, one that involves pushing yourself out of your comfort zone.

3. *Prepare yourself for fear, self-doubt, and low motivation*, as anyone who has reached the pinnacle of their discipline has felt self-doubt and unmotivated, and likely continues to have these feelings. They do not let this stop them.

Step 1. Identify What to Work On

The first step is to decide what you want to achieve. Think about an activity in which you want to improve. Here are some activity domains to consider:

» Interpersonal (relationships, public speaking, teaching, coaching, community building)

» Intrapersonal (meditation, spirituality, journaling, reading, self-compassion)

» Physical (sport and exercise)

» Intellectual (learning something new, mastering some intellectual domain)

» Technical (dance steps, building things, fixing things)

» Creative (visual arts, music, singing, cooking, gardening)

» Industry (running a business, managing people)

» Humanitarian (starting a charity, volunteering)

Now consider if the activity you want to work on speaks to how you want to live. If value underpins your action, then you are more likely to have sustained motivation over time.

Abandon empty busy-ness;
put your efforts into life-enhancing activities.

Think about the activity you want to strive for and then answer these questions:

1. Does the activity reflect the sort of person you want to be in your heart (not in appearances or social status)?
2. Is the activity a passion?
3. Does the activity bring meaning or purpose to your life?
4. Does the activity let you connect with others?
5. Is the activity in harmony with other aspects of your life?

To have sustained motivation, you'd want to answer yes to most of these questions. You don't want to put time into something that doesn't matter much to you; that's a certain path to demotivation.

Step 2. Develop a Deliberate Practice Plan

You may be stuck in the modern dilemma. Like most people, you probably feel overwhelmed by life sometimes. Too many obligations, too little time. Consider for a moment whether your energy is being directed to what you love. If the answer is no, it's time to change.

| Change the paradigm: Make time count.

Consider this analogy: Bishop is a competent chess player and spends thousands of hours playing speed chess, but his improvement lags. Bishop gets frustrated and thinks he needs some luck; maybe changing his name to King might help. Maybe that will help him win some games. Alas, random wishes won't allow him (or you) to improve. Bishop's problem is that merely playing or wishing doesn't work. Playing speed chess is comfortable and easy for him, but he doesn't study his errors. He plays a game, and then dashes to the next game.

To improve, he'll need to enter his discoverer space. Bishop needs to leave his habit zone, deliberately exposing himself to challenges he can't always handle. The habit zone is comfortable, but nothing much happens there. When out of the habit zone, Bishop will get feedback from his failures and setbacks as well as his wins. Research shows folks like Bishop will need to struggle to solve complex chess problems over and over, and lose games at chess tournaments over and over.[2] Five hours practicing in the uncomfortable zone is likely equal to twenty hours of comfy speed chess. Quality engagement is more critical than quantity.[3]

Over to you.

Consider the thing you'd like to achieve.

Now, engage in deliberate practice by using these three steps:

1. *Embrace the unknown.* To improve, you often need to do something new. For example, if you want to enhance work performance, you might seek a work coach. Or, if you're going to be more social and build your friendships, perhaps you'll investigate moving from online

tai chi classes to joining a local group. Stepping out of that habit zone into the unknown is growth. It sets your energy spinning toward value.

2. *Step boldly into life.* Next, set some goals that link to action. Consider what steps you'll do to develop your skill. Set goals in the sweet spot,[4] that's not too easy but not so hard that you feel frustrated, get burned out, or become injured. For example, if approaching a mentor feels too big, you might join an online discussion group in your field. If learning guitar, choose music that challenges you, something you can't *do in your sleep*, but not so hard that you get discouraged. Only you can decide where the challenge sweet spot is.

3. *Learn from your mistakes.* Pay attention to your results and measure how you are improving. For example, if you're joining a tai chi class, notice whether you're out of step, adjust your moves, and ask for feedback. If you are learning guitar, record yourself performing something now and record yourself a few weeks later. Listen to where you are improving and where you need to improve. Seek feedback from a teacher. Remind yourself that growth is about embracing feedback, not beating yourself up.

Step 3. Prepare for Fear, Self-Doubt, and Low Motivation

Mistakes will make you stronger. Assume that whenever you leave your habit zone and enter your discovery space, you will make mistakes. Deliberate practice isn't easy. You will lose your confidence, and your advisor will throw self-doubt at you. Remember, mistakes are the whole point of discovery. Self-doubt doesn't have to get in your way.

The next illustration shows you how achievement occurs. Each step up represents an improvement from deliberate practice or study. You can see that with steps toward achievement, your thoughts and feelings will change. Some days you'll feel confident, other days unmotivated or insecure. You don't have control over feelings and thoughts because when you push yourself to get better, you increase the risk of mistakes and setbacks, and therefore self-criticism. The thing you have control over is your practice. Keep showing up on your life path and have faith that deliberate efforts will elevate you. Keep moving your hands and feet toward your goals.

When fear and self-doubt get in the way, remember to return to the present moment. The most straightforward instruction in sports is, *Keep your eye on the ball.* There's a variation of this in most activities: *Really hear the music*

KEEP STEPPING FORWARD, EVEN AS YOU ENCOUNTER DISAPPOINTMENT, SELF-DOUBT, AND SETBACKS.

as you play it, or *forget the past game, focus on now*. When we learn new things or try to improve, we often have a head full of instructions—and we neglect to focus on the task. When you are not in the present, you become insensitive to the demands of the situation. You are also less aware of feedback and less able to learn. Thus, a critical skill for excellence is catching yourself when you have left the present moment and then returning.

It is said that breathing recalibrates the rhythm of the universe. As Timothy Gallwey writes in *The Inner Game of Tennis*, "When the mind is fastened to the rhythm of breathing, it tends to become absorbed and calm. Whether on or off the court, I know of no better way to begin to deal with anxiety than to place the mind on one's breathing process."[5] The simplest way to return to the present is to ground yourself by slowing your breath (see the exercises in chapter 3).

Breathing can help with achievement stress too, but the aim isn't to eliminate the stress. That's impossible. Attempting to eliminate all stress is another form of retreating to the habit zone. Learning, competing, and stretching yourself out of your habit zone comes with a certain amount of stress. You stress your body when you do resistance training or practice something difficult. You stress your mind when you are struggling to learn something new.

You'll also need recovery time after a stressful practice. So make sure you take rest days, engage in relaxing activities, eat well, and get enough sleep.

> There is no success without stress.

Achievers pay attention to stress in their bodies and detect when beneficial stress is tipping into harmful stress. Signs of too much stress include fatigue, irritability, agitation, feeling burned out, or seeing your outcomes decline. If this happens, it is time to rest.

> Stress and rest are two sides of the same coin.
> You need both to achieve.

Use Your Advisor as a Training Partner

Your advisor plays a role in your achievement. You need rules and instructions to tell you when you are beginning—*Stand behind the line when serving and return the ball inside the lines.* Your advisor can then internalize these rules to remind you, *Keep the ball inside the lines.* Once you improve, your advisor is no longer needed because you'll develop habits. It's like learning to drive a car. When you're a learner, there are multiple instructions all at once—look left, look right, indicate, then accelerate while slowly releasing the clutch—but once you have mastered driving, you barely think of these instructions. (Until you try teaching a new driver and realize how complicated it is.)

Once you become skilled, you increasingly get into a *flow state*, where you are absorbed in the task. A dancer in flow state does not need their advisor to say, *Left foot first, then point your toe.* They do it intuitively. These can become blissful moments in life, stepping into the flow and being present with an activity you value, with your advisor staying silent.

There is sometimes tension with your advisor and achievement. Your advisor is often helpful, but it can also interfere with complex behaviors. Let's take a look at Ann's example of when her advisor got in the way of her achievement.

I spent three years studying acting. After two years and playing several smaller roles, I was cast as the lead. I was excited but nervous. Like many creative or performance roles, I needed to be fully in the moment to be authentic and "real" on stage. So, the pressure was on. It was a weird paradox. In front of a paying audience, full of all my family, friends, and teachers who were assessing me, I had to let go of control. However, my advisor had other ideas. To protect me from the threat of failure, it decided to feed me instructions on exactly how to "let go": it reminded me to "be spontaneous," "listen authentically," and "look surprised." It was a disaster. I was robotic, artificial, and a failure on stage. My advisor's attempt to control my spontaneity ended up destroying it. Unfortunately, I never got another shot at playing a lead role after that. I still feel such shame when I recall this. But I've learned to not always let my advisor be in charge.

There are at least two instances where your advisor, or self-talk, is not useful for achievement. First, some things are too complex to put into words and are better understood through your body and practice memory than your self-talking advisor. Second, your advisor can harm achievement by focusing on task-irrelevant things.[6] During an activity, the last thing you want to do is worry about a future play or some past mistake. Peak achievement requires 100 percent focused energy.

This brings us back to those basic advisor steps in chapter 2.

1. *See it.* Notice when your advisor is helping *and* when it is distracting you or undermining your performance. If it is not helping, then go on to step 2.

2. *Redirect it, rather than resist it.* There is no need to fight your advisor or control your thoughts. Instead, shift into your noticer by pausing and taking a slow exhale. Gently shift your attention back to the task. Then move to the third step.

3. *Rule it (with rules of thumb).* Some self-talk *may* be useful in your quest to build expertise.[7] Your self-talk should focus on the present moment, not dwell on past mistakes or future outcomes. For example, it would probably be unhelpful to tell yourself, *Don't keep making the same dumb mistakes.* This shifts energy away from the present, where it is most needed. Make sure your advisor statements work for you. Here are some examples, but remember to create your own unique rules. Practice self-talk that is useful *to you*:

   Increase motivation—You can do this! Hang in there. Remain strong.

   Increase acceptance of hard experiences—Self-doubt is a normal part of getting better.

Suggest effective strategy—Slow down and breathe (when rushing). Stay calm.

Get into the present moment—Focus on this step.

Focus on particular skills—Hit with more topspin.

*Use **when-then** expressions*—When I am feeling tired, then I will push one more repetition, and then stop.

Practicing to Achieve

The practice steps in this chapter will help you stay in balance as you work toward your goals. Practice keeping yourself on an even keel, neither overchallenged nor underchallenged.

Achieving self

Identify what to work on and link it to value.	Deliberate practice: Embrace unknown, take bold action steps, learn from mistakes, balance stress and rest.	Use noticer to focus and advisor as your training partner.

Over-challenged:
Challenges too hard, high stress, too little rest, challenge not value driven.

Under-challenged:
Challenges too easy, stop striving whenever feel doubt or unmotivated, avoid leaving comfort zone.

Chapter 9

YOUR PROFOUND AWARENESS

Peace is not the absence of stress; peace is found within your awareness practice.

Every morning the sun rises and the world transforms, darkness fades and you barely remember its shadow. Possibility returns. Birds celebrate this moment with song, sensing the power of dawn. You too have this transformational power. One moment you're standing in the dark of dawn, struggling to breathe, fighting negative thoughts, tired of life—then just a small action can bring light. Perhaps you greet the sun, say hello to your fellow commuter, say yes to that job, or hit the sign-up button on that painting course you've yearned to do. These small moments take you forward. They open awareness inside you.

These moments are the focus of this chapter. You will learn how to capture small changes within and use them to open your life anew. As you work through this chapter, you'll see vitality is never lost; it always lies a step away. A sliding door from struggle to peacefulness. Do not turn away from the change. Birds do not deny the dawn their song, and neither should you. Stay. Then you'll discover the brilliance of living with possibility.

This chapter introduces three practices that guide you down the path toward profound awareness. Each practice has instructions and an accompanying recording for download at http://dnav.international. With them, you can increase your presence, obtain peacefulness, even improve your concentration and achievements. With practice, your new superpower can become equanimity, the ability to be calm in any storm.

Releasing the Struggle

Before we present these practices, let's first discuss why practice is so essential. The world has changed you. You've lived so long now, that *what you have experienced* can be mistaken for *who you are*. For example, if you've been victimized, you might think you *are* a victim. If you failed at something, you might think you *are* a failure. Not so. You *experienced* a past—you don't have to become it.

When you were born, you were like clear water. Think of your history as like tea leaves dropped into the water, transforming the color, taste, and smell. Yet the water remains; it's always within the tea. Just as your clear self remains too.

The world presented you with challenges and problems, and you fought and clawed your way to solutions. You educated yourself, built friendships and love, found employment, and overcame all the hassles of daily life—paying bills, doing your laundry, getting to work on time, managing difficulties with other people, etc. Your brain and body reacted to each of these modern-day challenges by dumping fight-or-flight chemicals into your bloodstream. Whenever you overcame a problem, those chemicals dissipated, and you relaxed and were rewarded with feel-good chemicals like dopamine. However, if you've been in constant fight-and-flight mode, being in a relaxed state can feel like a problem. It's as if you have let your guard down, and danger may now enter unseen. When was the last time you relaxed without that creeping feeling that you *should* get something done?

Don't lose sight of what's still within you. As an infant, you once giggled with pure joy just because someone smiled at you. That pureness—that wholehearted openness to the moment—is still within. If you practice, you can let it rise again. You can see the world as good, at least sometimes. You can learn to see your body as good too. You can open your advisor to new ideas. You can discover that life has more. You can see other people as good. It takes practice to be sure. But you *can* enjoy experience as it is, not as your mind says it is, clouded by life's struggles. Experience is there in the blue of the sky, the chill of fresh rain, the eyes of your loved one, or the feel of a hug. The capacity is within you.

Practice the Right Thing

Are you aware that you practice your psychological state until it becomes your habit? It goes like this: If you practice being stressed, your habit zone is stressing. If you practice being peaceful, then peacefulness will become your habit. Behavioral research shows your thoughts, feelings, and actions all follow this basic reinforcement paradigm.[1] Worry is a clear example. Let's say you worry a lot about your job. You think about it when you're awake and asleep. Each time you worry, you are reinforcing yourself for *seemingly doing something* about the problem. But it's a trap. Worrying doesn't change your job situation, it merely *seems like it helps*, but it costs you the present and puts you firmly inside a habit zone that you probably don't want.

These behavioral reinforcement principles share similar conclusions to centuries-old contemplative practices. For example, 2,500 years ago, Gautama Buddha began his introspective experiments in the hope of discovering the secrets of human suffering. He put his questions to the test through decades of deep meditation, introspection, and debate—and he too came to the insight that your everyday experience is dependent on what you practice. Suffering is greater when our habit is struggling with it. Peace is greater when we practice that too.

Ask yourself, then, what is your usual psychological state? With practice, you can create a new life where doubt and fear don't dominate, because you practice letting them come and go. You long for peace, so you practice it. If you don't, how will you get peaceful?

Practices to Create Your Indestructible Self

Move into the discoverer zone now. Imagine yourself as you were before all your experiences changed you. Step aside from your labels, judgments, evaluations, and habits, and see that you were once whole and able to *just be*. You probably never think of yourself as whole and complete. Yet, you can probably look at a newborn infant and see them that way. We invite you to begin by entertaining the notion that there is an indestructible part of you, even if it's hard to see.

This indestructible, grounded self is waiting to grow through the practice we describe now. There's neuroscience evidence to show that meditation practices like the ones we describe can change your brain within weeks.[2] With just a small investment of time each day, you can develop greater equanimity, learning to be level-headed and calm in any storm.

The right kind of practice and your intention matter. You don't want to practice to become a better employee or a better cog in the machine. We are not advocating the type of mindfulness that's superficial, devoid of purpose, groundless, and can increase selfishness. That is sometimes called McMindfulness,[3] and it doesn't have the same beneficial effects as the practice we're advocating in this chapter. Here we use meditation practices informed by centuries-old wisdom traditions.[4] We're not advocating for any type of religion. Our aim is to help you develop good practice actions that allow you to see your grounded self and your interdependence in all humanity.

> You practice to find your whole self,
> to release yourself into profound awareness,
> and to connect to the interdependence of all beings.

Experiencing Equanimity

Our first meditative practice has six steps to build your awareness and capacity for equanimity. This is based on calm abiding practice, and adapted from the teachings of Pema Khandro.[5] Follow each step explicitly, without leaving any steps out or taking any shortcuts. It will require you to dedicate 10 minutes per day for 21 days. That's just 3.5 hours of your life. Try not to miss a day, but if you do, just pick up where you left off. At the end of 21 days, you *will be* changed.

The six essential steps are described below. They are recorded on audio too, so don't worry if it seems like a lot to take in by reading.[6]

Note, some readers with trauma histories may require *trauma-informed* meditation. You can still try our practices below but do trust your experience. If you feel unsafe, pause and seek out professional help.

Six Steps to Effective Practice

1. Create a dedicated time and place for your meditation practice.
2. Begin with purpose.
3. Prepare your body.
4. State your valued intention.
5. Practice using an evidence-based method.
6. End with a dedication or motivation.

Let's look at what each of these steps entails.

1. **Create a dedicated time and place for your meditation practice.**
The hardest part about meditation is remembering to do it. We plan to, but then each day slips by, and we've forgotten it. To overcome this, we plan where, when, and how long.

Where. You don't need an out of the way meditation room; just create a peaceful corner in any room and place a few reminders for visual cues to *trigger* your mind and body. You'll walk past it, and that cushion/chair/picture will be calling out to you, *C'mon, time to meditate*.

When. Choose a consistent time. Mornings are often ideal, because you're in a liminal state, between awake and asleep. Plus, you haven't had coffee or lots of stimulation yet. It's okay if that doesn't suit you; choose another time, but try to make it a transition time, such as between home and work. Then, set a reminder on your device. Note that bedtime generally isn't the best time because you'll likely be sleepy, and that's the opposite of practicing awareness.

How long. Use a timer, so you won't be thinking, *How much longer?* Five minutes is great to start. If 5 minutes of practice seems too long, an interval chime at 2.5 minutes can help, because you know you're halfway.

2. Begin with purpose.

A meditation session should begin purposefully; it's part of the practice. If you rush in, you're likely to have a busy mind and rush to get it over. That negates the entire purpose. So, as you begin, take a few seconds to establish and honor your practice. You can count this in your minutes too, if you like.

Take a slow seat, ring a bell, or light a candle.

These actions will trigger you—*it's time to practice*. Remember, learning by consequences becomes a habit.

3. Prepare your body.

You will be more effective at tuning in if you follow a body settling routine. This also counts as part of your time. These steps cue your body that *it's time to put your worries aside and practice*. When you meditate, you should be comfortable. It should not cause physical pain.

Follow this seven-point posture, moving your awareness from toes to head in order.

1. *Legs*—Find a comfortable cross-legged position (if sitting on a chair, have your bottom pushed to the back of the chair and your feet flat on the floor or on a box).

2. **Hips**—Use a firm cushion to tilt your hips forward, so your hips are higher than your knees; this way, your legs are less likely to go numb.

3. **Spine**—Straighten your spine, so it is comfortable and erect, and soften your belly.

4. **Shoulders**—Rest your shoulders out and down.

5. **Hands**—Rest your hands on your thighs or place your right palm over your left and rest them in your lap.

6. **Face**—Soften your jaw and relax your face.

7. **Eyes**—Keep your eyes partially open with a soft gaze resting on a spot in front of you. In meditation statues you'll notice the eyes are partly open and that's because it's a good way to learn. Eyes partly open keeps you alert, whereas eyes closed can set your mind racing or give you light flashing behind your lids.

Settle in by saying each marker to trigger your habit—*legs-hips-spine-shoulders-hands-face-eyes*.

4. State your valued intention.

You want meditation to be meaningful, not just one more task in your day. Remind yourself that you are practicing because you long for something, so your intention should be aspirational and linked to value. Quietly say your intention out loud. It might follow the formula below, or it can be unique to you.

I practice meditation (action) to build peace in myself and others (aspirational value) and accept that I don't control what comes.

I practice for greater peace; I accept that peace is something that comes and goes.

I practice now so that I and those I love may be free of suffering.

5. Practice using an evidence-based method.

Once you're sufficiently prepared, you can choose one technique below to practice.

Thinking—Focus your attention on your exhale. Don't change your inhale. Just settle your awareness on each exhale. When you lose track of your exhales, merely label this as "thinking" and return to being aware of your breath.

Counting—Focus your attention on each exhale, counting each exhale from 1 to 20 and then back down to 1, and repeat. If you lose track of counting, just restart at 1 as many times as you need to.

Chanting—Follow your inhale, pause, and then exhale and link each part of breathing to a silent chant:

- **Silently repeating 1, 2, 3**—1 (in-breath), 2 (pause), 3 (long out-breath).

- **Chanting Om Ah Hung**—*Om* (in-breath), *Ah* (pause), *Hung* (out-breath).[7]

As you try these steps, remember the purpose of meditation isn't to control or stop thinking; it is to help you train your attention from its constant flitter and distraction to a deeper, more profound presence. If you get distracted, remind yourself that it's normal. Distraction is what minds do. You will get distracted many times in five minutes, even many times in five seconds. There is no need to get upset. When you realize you have lost concentration, gently bring your awareness back to one of the methods above.

Finally, remember that it will take consecutive days of practice to see the benefits. How many days depends on the individual, but 21 days is an excellent beginning commitment that can show effects.

6. **End with a dedication or motivation.**
Create some positive energy for your day, your world, and others. At the end of each meditation, dedicate your practice with a brief statement:

May we be happy.
May we find peace.
May the benefits for myself and others be shared.

This meditation practice will help you begin cultivating a sense of awareness of your indestructible self. Let's look at the next two methods.

So far in this book, you have seen how your words, labels, thoughts, and descriptions can stick to you. In this practice you will see the nature of thoughts as they unfold and practice being grounded to the you that is present here and now. Words and thoughts are elusive. You know how it is when you dream—your cognitions can be wild and fantastical. You might dream that you are riding a unicorn across Middle Earth or that your house is burning down. No matter what the dream, when you wake, you know you were dreaming, and you let it go. It may take effort or perhaps time if it's emotional, but you still do know how to let a dream pass.

You're the dreamer, not the dream.

Have you ever wondered why you treat day thoughts so differently? What if your daytime thoughts were also empty of realness—that is, until you follow them, believe them, or act on them? Knowing that reality isn't in your thoughts and feelings can liberate you. Perhaps if you can allow a dream to come and go, then you can do the same with a thought, even a nasty one. Of course, it is challenging to do. But with practice, you can create a new life where your thoughts and feelings do not rule you.

Here the practice is becoming so flexible with a thought that you choose what to do with it. You'll begin to see thinking as a tool, using it when it's helpful, letting it pass when it isn't.

Practice Seeing Words as Empty

Try this super brief mindfulness practice:

1. Focus your awareness on something in the natural world—a tree, the sky, etc. We'll use the example of a tree for ease of explanation.

2. Now release one long slow exhale.

3. Evaluate the tree as good by considering all the good things about this tree.

4. Then, evaluate the tree as bad, seeing all of its negative aspects.

5. Notice that no matter what labels, thoughts, or evaluations you give that tree, the tree is just there being a tree. It doesn't care, and it doesn't change.

6. Your profound awareness is like this. Positive and negative self-evaluations come and go. Your profound self stays the same.

Try practicing this short mindfulness exercise and letting evaluations go. Remind yourself of this new advisor rule: *You're the thinker, not the thought.*

Finally, let's explore the third practice, which is opening up to your embodied awareness so that you can truly accept your physical self.

Re-envision Your Body as Good

First, consider how you see your body as *labels*: fat, thin, old, ill, abused. You see your body as *objectified parts* too, e.g., having a good nose, a fat belly, or great legs. Make no mistake, though: none of these evaluations *is* your body. These evaluations are conditioned ways of seeing it and are all based on your learning history. With practice, you can allow the labels and objectifications to fall away and learn to see your body in its true form, as a presence and power.

| Your body is a presence and power.

One way to experience your body's power is by being aware of it during novel or peak experiences—when you cross the finish line of a 5k run, when you step onto the peak after a long day hiking, when you hug a loved one after a long break apart, or when you have a profound yoga or meditation session. Imagine a moment like that now:

1. Breathe and recall a peak moment.

2. Just notice what that moment feels like in your body.

3. This is when your body is experienced as good enough, when it is a presence instead of a label or an object.

Other peak experiences give you a sense of vulnerability, such as experiencing a sudden injury, being ill, even giving birth. Imagine a moment like that now:

1. Breathe and recall a moment of vulnerability.

2. In these moments, your body is telling you the power of its presence.

Your body is not a label. These exercises reveal your body as a sensitive, profound presence. Since the moment of your birth, you have been in your body to experience pleasure and pain.

Practice accepting your body.

Here is a practice where you can be open to fully experiencing life through your body instead of your labels or parts.

Breathe and notice your heart beating.
Say, *I will not see my body as negative.*

Breathe and connect with your noticer, your pure ability to sense the world.
Say, *I will not see my body through my conditioning.*

Breathe and notice your chest rise.
Say, *I will not see my body in a degrading way.*

You connect with the best experiences of your life through your embodied noticer. It's freeing to experience your body as being okay, just as it is, even with the scars and battles of a lifetime on it. Sit quietly for a few moments and allow your senses to wash over you.

Practicing to Experience Profound Awareness

Profound awareness is possible for you, it just takes practice. Each day, practice to see your body and mind as whole. Meditation practices will help you become aware of when you are pushing away internal states or clinging to a special state, and help you return to center.

Your profound awareness

Become aware of your indestructible grounded presence.

Re-envision your self-talk as empty.

Deliberate practice using 6 steps.

Re-envision your body as good.

Pushing away: Avoiding emotions or difficult thoughts and experiences. Disconnected from grounded-self.

Clinging: Should always be happy, must have positive states, cannot have bad things happen. Disconnected from grounded-self.

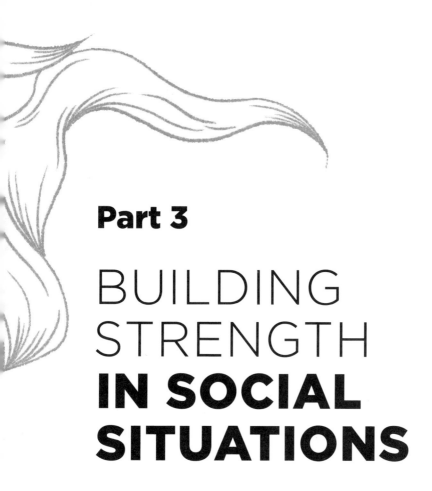

Part 3

BUILDING STRENGTH IN SOCIAL SITUATIONS

To love and be loved is our greatest desire
and our greatest challenge.

"When we really look closely, the world of stuff and advertising is not really life. Life is the other stuff. Life is what is left when you take all that crap away, or at least ignore it for a while. Life is the people who love you. No one will ever choose to stay alive for an iPhone. It's the people we reach via the iPhone that matter. And once we begin to recover, and to live again, we do so with new eyes. Things become clearer, and we are aware of things we weren't aware of before."

—Matt Haig, *Reasons to Stay Alive*[1]

We have arrived now to the heart center of life, your social connections. People you connect with and care for will be your greatest source of joy and meaning. We hope to honor this because helping you strengthen your social world matters deeply to us too.

We've called this section "social strength," which means being able to create friendship, love, and strong connections, as well as being able to steer through the darkness of suffering, social conflict, and difficulties with other people. We devote the final section to this because we know that you'll thrive with stronger social groups. Being alone and being human are incompatible. Loneliness comes with loss, anxiety, sadness, and a raft of health issues.[2] Social conflict comes with struggle and affects your success at work.[3] You might struggle a lot, as many of us do, because social intelligence is rarely taught explicitly. Think about that. You've spent years learning in formal education and in your work, but how many courses have you taken on developing your ability to be stronger socially? You might be an expert in your job, but if nobody supports you, it won't matter much. Your greatest social struggles will come from not knowing what to do, or continuing to fumble and repeat the same missteps, or not trying new social strategies. You can keep seeking to improve your social world, even when you get stuck, and these chapters can help. Join us on the journey to increase your social strength and build strong social alliances, friendships, and intimate relationships.

 **Chapter 10**

CHANGING TO A FLEXIBLE SOCIAL STYLE

Seek to please everyone, and you lose respect; judge and dismiss people, and you lose friendships. Find the middle way, which balances your desire to not be hurt with your need to build trusting relationships.

f you had to live on an unpopulated island, what would you take with you? Would you take your favorite possession or your favorite person? Simple choice, right? Your favorite person. Knowing this leads us to a central paradox. We value people more than anything in this world, yet we find it hard to get along. Think of all the challenges you've experienced with other people: families fighting, relationships ending, coworkers backstabbing—the list goes on. Why is it so hard to get along, given that it is so important?

One reason is that we bring our history into our present relationships. It can feel as if the current relationship will be like past relationships. If, for example, someone has mistreated you in the past, you might respond to new people with distrust and avoidance. We all have old coping styles, and you're not to blame here. Often these old coping styles influence—even dictate—how you behave in your relationships. Sometimes you end up getting the opposite of what you want; for example, you seek connection only to find yourself defensive and guarded, which leads to disconnection. These patterns continue because they're outside your awareness.

This chapter will help you identify your social patterns and how they can influence your relationships in unhelpful ways. Then we'll show you how to develop a flexible social style, one that allows you to get closer to others or create distance, depending on what builds social value in your life.

Social Styles

Family life shapes our social styles.[1] Let's do an exercise where you reflect on your family history and see the social styles that you developed. Go slow and imagine. Perhaps put this book aside for a moment as you consider each question. There is no rush.

Identify Your Social Style

1. Imagine yourself at eight to twelve years old (or later, if you can't recall this young). To get you in to your sense of this time, first see if you can remember a teacher from elementary school, and then see if you can recall a childhood friend.

2. Picture your family at home or the home where you grew up. What was it like to live there? Can you still see it?

3. Now, notice how you felt in your family or with the people you lived with. Did you feel anxious? Were people moody or absent? Were people emotionally intense, often yelling, or quiet and emotionally restrained?

4. What did your parents or caregivers do when you were sad, angry, or anxious? Were they available to coach you and show you how to have those feelings? Did they shut you down or ignore you?

5. Who would you turn to for emotional support, and how would that person respond? For example, who would you turn to if you felt scared, and what would they do?

6. How might all of these things impact your relationship style now?

These early life relationships affect your connection patterns and play an important role in your adult relationships.[2] There are four patterns we might learn.[3] Read through each description below, and as you do, consider whether any style describes how you usually interact. You may see yourself as a blend of styles, too.

1.   **The secure style.** I find it easy to get close to others, and I am comfortable with them depending on me. I am worthy of support and love and seek to build trusting relationships.

2.   **The anxious style.** I often seek reassurance from others. I recognize the value of being close with another person, but I fear I care for them more than they care for me.

3.   **The avoidant style.** I fear others may devalue me, hurt me, or abuse my trust. I avoid getting too close so that I don't get hurt.

4.   **The dismissing style.** I distrust others and don't think I can depend on them. I focus on independence and self-sufficiency.

Consider the illustration on the next page. It depicts the four styles. If you have an *anxious* style, you get worried about your interactions, double-checking and making sure your close connections are okay and that they're not upset with you. In doing so, you may neglect your own needs and self-care. If you have an *avoidant* style, you might keep yourself closed and avoid the issues, so you don't get hurt, but your relationship might miss out on the honesty and openness that comes through sharing. If you have a *dismissing* style, you prefer to walk away. You try to be independent and self-sufficient. Anxious, avoiding, and dismissing are socially inflexible styles and will sometimes stop you from building solid relationships and authentic connections.

Our goal throughout this book is to help you become more psychologically flexible. In terms of relationships, this is acting more in the *secure* style of responding. This is when you can discuss, share, have different views, and remain confident that you can have a trusting, intimate relationship. You are also confident enough to walk away from a relationship that is not working. Don't worry if that's not you now. We are all a work in progress.

SECURE

ANXIOUS

AVOIDANT

DISMISSIVE

To help you see how these styles play out in life, we share an example from Joseph that we hope will help you see how these styles repeat themselves. For some readers, this may be a distressing childhood story, and it may trigger your memories too. Use your noticer ability if you need to, pause, and breathe. We are with you.

My dad hated me. That's how it felt. I was, as he once told me, a weight around his neck. He had not wanted to have me. My mother had supposedly tricked him into having me, and then when she left, he was stuck with me. If it weren't for me, he might have met someone he loved, or been able to get a good job, or finished university earlier. Everything I did seemed to irritate him.

I recall when I was about twelve, Dad was learning psychology at university. I knew this because he kept giving me intelligence tests.

One day he said to me, "Name a type of meat."

He was in one of those angry, intimidating moods. I heard the question but my mind blanked.

"Come on. What's wrong with you?" he said, raising his voice.

I sat frozen.

"Soap," I finally said.

"Soap?" he growled. "Soap is meat? Then go to the bathroom and eat soap. Go now! Go!"

I remember standing next to the toilet nibbling on soap. Then words came flooding into me: hot dogs, hamburger, steak. I had known the answer. Why did I blank?

Fear eventually turned to anger. *I hate him*, I thought. *Someday, I'll leave. I don't care what he thinks.*

Today, I see my pattern; I would get angry and dismiss my father: he was the enemy.

Fast-forward twenty years. I was driving my date to a restaurant and trying to impress her, but I got nervous and soon was lost on a dark road. I pulled over and tried to read a map. My date squirmed. It was our first date, and she didn't know me. She was getting nervous, and I realized she was about to end the date. I couldn't focus on the map. Then, as if from nowhere, I thought, *Ditch her before she ditches you.*

"You know, you don't really know me. I could be a mass murderer," I blurted out, in probably the single worst line anybody ever said while parked on a dark road with an almost stranger.

She laughed politely, but her eyes widened. "Can you please take me home?"

I've screwed up again, I told myself, as I drove her home. The old question returned: *Will I ever find someone who loves me?*

Today, I realize I was dismissing her just as I did my father.

Joseph had developed a dismissive attachment style. This protected him from an abusive father. It worked as a child, but it was not working as a young adult. His dismissing style interfered with his ability to find love and friendship. Over the years, he has worked to change his style and build a more secure style. He can't erase his old learning, though, and he still has the urge to dismiss when stressed, but he has learned to notice the urge and not react to it. By not immediately dismissing, he has increased his chances of genuinely connecting with people.

Does your earlier learning creep in and leave you responding in ways that you don't want? Do you repeat anxious, avoidant, or dismissing styles, even when they stand in the way of what you want? For example, imagine a romantic partner has hurt you in some deep way, perhaps ended the relationship. Although you want another intimate relationship, you don't want to be hurt again either, so you decide to protect yourself. From then on, you hide your emotions and keep your guard up, assuming every new relationship will be dangerous. Everyone can hurt you if you let your guard down. Consequently, you never get close to anyone, and you never build a secure relationship. In this example, your social style would stop you from finding genuine connections.

....

Make Pausing a New Habit

A hermit crab must leave its shell to search for a bigger shell to call home. As it is leaving the shell, unprotected, soft, and vulnerable, do you think it feels fear? Would it hesitate just a little longer in the shell? Just another day. Sure, its shell is uncomfortable, but it *feels* safe. Your old social styles can be like that shell. They are familiar, but you may have outgrown them. To gradually change your social style, you need to practice new styles of responding until they become your new home, a new place to inhabit.

Once you see what your pattern is, you can learn new responses by interrupting yourself. Your aim is to respond with awareness instead of automaticity. You'll practice slowing yourself down, creating space so you can form new ways of interacting and achieving the connection you desire. The key to interrupting your pattern isn't *to stop* your feelings and urges, but to use your noticer ability instead and see those feelings and urges without reacting to them. You want *pausing* to become a new habit. We use the word *habit* to remind you that this process will take practice. When you are in the heat of a disagreement, you'll tend to respond habitually: perhaps dismiss, argue, or seek reassurance. Something familiar. You'll react and realize afterward that you acted in a way that produced the outcome you least wanted—disconnection and disappointment.

You can practice your new habit right now.

Practice Pausing

In a moment of interaction, try not to react immediately. Pause. Take a breath. Notice your urge to respond in your old style. Do this a few times in everyday interactions. Once you pause and notice *in the moment of connection*, you become freer to vary your responses. You have given yourself a breath of time, and this is your opportunity to create change.

Practice Pausing in Difficult Moments

To practice the pausing ability during moments of difficulty, try this exercise. Go slowly and sink into the experience.

1. Think of someone with whom you want to deepen your relationship. Think of what it's like to be with them and what you like about spending time together.

2. Now, think of a time you disagreed. Think of a specific event. Take your time and get immersed in the memory.

3. Now, see yourself from the observer perspective. Step back and see yourself disagreeing with the other person. Feel your urge to react in the old way. What do you feel an urgency to do? Do you want to seek reassurance and smooth it over (anxious style), remove yourself because it hurts (avoidant style), or dismiss them and argue (dismissive style)? Perhaps it's a confusing mix of all of these.

4. Ask yourself whether this happens a lot when you interact with people you care about. Is this urge familiar to you? Try not to blame yourself here; instead, remind yourself that you are practicing awareness.

When you are ready, try practicing in a heated moment. Pause. Notice your urge to respond. It can help to use your noticing-inside ability here too: notice your feet on the ground, and wriggle your toes if you need to. Try noticing-outside, too, perhaps becoming aware of the sounds around you.

Next, use your advisor to remind you of a new self-rule. Try saying to yourself, *Step back, slow down.*

Then notice your breath. Be aware if your body is tipping into any unbalanced states, like those we described in chapter 5. If you notice you are stressing out or shutting down, step away and rebalance yourself.

If you need more practice, revisit the strategies from the earlier chapters, specifically noticer, vulnerable self, and compassionate self.

Choose Valued Action

Once you have pressed pause on your habitual style, you are ready for something new. Use your valuer here; it is perhaps the most important aspect in relationships. You'll always need to consider value from two perspectives: your value in the relationship and your value of self-care. Your aim is to balance both. Here's what that looks like.

Your Value in the Relationship

Ask yourself, what matters to you in this relationship? Is there a value in building it or staying in it?

If you answer yes, then consider what kind of person you want to be during difficulties. Do you want to be supportive? Do you want to build closeness? Do you want to connect?

Next, ask yourself whether your actions in a tough moment are consistent with your value. If they aren't, that's your signal to change and try a more value-consistent response. Note that you are not trying to erase your initial urge here; you can't eliminate habits quickly, and that's why your first response is to pause and practice noticing.

Consider a different response. How might you respond in new or different ways so that you build your connection goal? You might try acting opposite to your habitual pattern; for example, if you automatically defend yourself, you might choose to listen and wait. You might try taking the other person's perspective, stepping into their shoes and seeking to understand their position and the shared value you have. You might try staying open and balanced; for example, if you become aware that you are shifting toward stress, try reminding yourself of the shared value in the relationship, and connect in that way. Finally, you might buy time by seeking some time to reflect and come back later to discuss the issue. Once you start thinking like this, you will create other ideas that are consistent with your value and the situation. Your aim is to seek a new action and test whether it leads to a stronger connection rather than old outcomes of disconnection and disappointment. Give yourself time to choose an action that will help your goals of connecting, rather than hindering them.

Your Value of Self-Care

Every relationship involves a constant balance between your needs and the other person's needs. If you think only of yourself, you'll appear selfish and incapable of intimacy. If you think only of others, you risk being abused and treated like a doormat. Balance comes from working on *both* your value and the other person's values.

There is no rigid, unchanging rule about how you can value yourself or others; rather, you need to stay flexible. Sometimes you will put others first; sometimes, you will put yourself first; sometimes, you and the other person's needs will be in perfect balance. Being flexible means you'll balance the seesaw between valuing yourself and others, moving it constantly up and down; you'll avoid sticking at one extreme, either putting yourself last all the time or putting yourself first all the time. A red flag is when your needs and values are always last or not considered at all. For example, if someone is narcissistic, they will ignore your needs. That is a sign to protect and care for yourself, not work on balance.

Being flexible means you persist in a good relationship, even when it is hard. Valuing self-care means you trust yourself and know that when a relationship no longer brings value, it's time to put yourself first.

Practicing a Flexible Social Style

Begin to strengthen your relationships by practicing the steps below.

Changing to a flexible social style

| Recognize your usual social style. | Practice pausing before "typical" response. | Choose valued actions that balance self and other. |

Over exposed:
Trying to please everyone and get everyone to like you.

Over protected:
Not letting anyone in or rejecting intimacy.

Chapter 11

BRINGING MORE LOVE AND FRIENDSHIP INTO YOUR LIFE

Give your gift of empathy, and you'll receive back the warmth of love.

Holding the phone to her ear, Talia poured a glass of wine and willed her friend to pick up.

Three rings. Four rings. Five.

"Oh, hey, Talia, how's it going?" Kim answered warmly.

"Hi," Talia said. "I'm okay . . . just saying hi."

Kim sensed something was wrong. "I'm okay" meant "I'll cry if I have to talk."

Talia talked about everyday stuff, lunch at work, what was on Instagram. Kim followed her lead, despite her urge to ask her friend what was wrong.

After a few minutes, Kim thought, *Now maybe I can ask.*

"What's up, Talia?" Kim asked. "You sound really stressed."

Talia unraveled. She talked about her boss and the pressure of work and feeling overwhelmed. All the while, Kim listened, matching her tone, following her feelings, imagining herself in Talia's shoes.

"What a crappy situation," Kim said. "That sucks. I wish you didn't have to go through this."

Talia nodded to herself.

"I'm here for you, Talia," Kim said. "You know you can call me anytime."

"I know. Thanks."

Talia knew Kim couldn't fix the problem but felt relief knowing her friend was there. When she hung up, she carried the warmth of their connection. Talia felt stronger.

Love is the glue that binds your well-being to that of others. Talia and Kim show the love between friends; as one struggles, the other steps up. You build love and connection this way, through showing empathy, being present, and valuing the relationship. In this chapter, we discuss how to develop nurturing relationships. You'll learn the empathy skills that build and grow genuine connection and love. Kim knew how to listen and provide warm, empathic responses. She knew how to read her friend's need for support without giving advice or trying to solve Talia's problem for her.

We describe two sets of actions that affect how well you support and connect with your loved ones. We'll also show you how to care for yourself in close relationships. You can do things to strengthen connection, such as being empathetic, and you can do things to hurt connection, such as trying to be right all the time. Sometimes you can do both in the same day. We will show you how to do more of the former and less of the latter. Dive in, and your relationships can flourish. Your loved ones will feel held and supported, and in return, you will receive love and connection.

Connection Is Your Lifeline

You are made for love. When you gaze into a young child's eyes and feel the urge to nurture and keep them safe, nature's forces are at work within you. Evolutionary processes drive a species to get what it needs for survival. In humans, that need is other people. As infants, we are too weak to find food, shelter, and safety alone, so we've adapted to rely on each other. Connection is deep within our cells. Disconnection will create pain. If someone excludes us, we will show the same pattern of neural activity in our brains as a physical injury.[1] Ask a loving couple to hold hands while one of them undergoes an electric shock and the pain of the shock will be reduced.[2] Inside the brains of this hand-holding couple, the pain centers will fire in mirrored patterns. We literally feel each other's pain.

And if we are alone, we die early. A longitudinal study followed adult males from nineteen years old until their nineties.[3] Whether they came from rich or poor backgrounds, one factor was consistently associated with well-being—good relationships. Fame, riches, and success did not drive their well-being; it came from deep connections with family, friends, and social groups. When we don't have relationships, our loneliness is a significant risk factor for premature death, equivalent to risks brought on by obesity, smoking, and air pollution.[4]

Literature, poetry, and art have never lost sight of the power of connection, but science and economics have. Modern societies have emphasized everything else as important—*above* authentic relationships. During your education, you were probably told grades and knowledge mattered most. Even today, your workplace might push hard on aspects like growing a brand, getting promoted, and building your skills without ever asking after your social needs. Modern technology allows you to work almost constantly, a human machine alone at a workstation. Advertisements tell you that you need products to have status and value. You are taught to value everything but love. Yet without love and trust, life has little purpose.

Individual wealth and material possessions have little influence on your happiness.[5] In contrast, social ties will influence your happiness, activity levels, and feelings of hope, sadness, or stress.[6] As the great poet John Donne argued,[7] nobody is an island entire of itself. If active, happy people surround you, then you will be active and happy, too. It's like their energy spreads to you and yours to them. You are part of a greater whole—you *and* your people.

Strengthening Your Connections

Empathy is the practice you need to strengthen your connections. It is the ability to step into another's shoes and *feel with* them. The ability helps you establish and maintain supportive relationships,[8] enables you to provide timely help to others,[9] and promotes cooperation in groups.[10]

Empathy is the ability of the socially intelligent, and yet few people learn empathy directly. You can mistakenly think being empathetic means giving in to the other person's needs, or giving sympathy, or telling your experience. Too often, we assume people will simply acquire the ability. We don't teach it in schools. We don't teach it to couples unless they come to therapy. And we don't teach it to young adults as a key friendship factor.

Here we show you how to improve your empathy. Empathy has two distinct aspects: warm empathy and cognitive empathy.[11] Let's learn how to do them both.

HOLDING THE EMPATHY BALL.

LIFE CAN FEEL HEAVY AND OVERWHELMING. FRIENDSHIP LIGHTENS THE LOAD.

Warm Empathy Is Always First

Begin by *feeling with*. There is probably nothing as powerful as seeing someone's pain and sharing it. Think of this practice as playing a game where your job is to catch the *empathy ball* and hold it. The other person is facing a struggle, so they throw their pain at you in a bid to get help—your task is to catch their struggle but not throw it back. In other words, don't share your knowledge or experience just yet. Take in what is happening and try to hold their message. It's their turn now—it'll be your turn later.[12]

Once you've become aware that empathy might be beneficial, try these actions:

1. **Pause** and become aware that the other person has something bothering them or something they want to tell you.
2. **Listen** as they tell you what is happening for them, and provide social encouragers, like nodding and eye contact. Listen with your ears, not

your mouth; don't interrupt and don't use your advisor to problem solve.

3. **Feel** with them. If your body was like theirs, how would you be standing? What would your posture be like? If it seems okay, you can even mirror them slightly, too, just to sense their experience. For example, if they slump down, you might slump a little too. Meet them in the same space.

4. **Sense** their breathing. Are they calm, or is their heart racing?

5. **Imagine** how they are feeling by trying to imagine how you might feel in their position.

Cognitive Empathy Is Always Second

After you've used warm, embodied empathy and good listening, you can move to cognitive empathy. This involves understanding the other person's experience cognitively, bringing your advisor in, and taking their perspective. These steps show you the process.

1. **Ask clarifying questions:** Tell me some more. What was that like for you? What were you hoping for?

2. **Check that you have all of their experience:** Is there more I should know?

3. **Validate and speak from the heart:** It's your turn to share only when you have all their information. Speak from your heart, sharing your views, if appropriate or necessary. Remind yourself of the value you share with this person. Ask, *How can I validate what they might feel and show them I care?*

4. **Problem solve or evaluate:** Do this only if they ask for it. Check first. Do you want me to help you with this, or do you want my opinion?

If you practice these empathy actions, people in your social circle will probably feel heard, held, and safe in your presence. Empathy can *seem* to take a long time, but it probably isn't as difficult as leaving your loved one feeling unheard and descending into arguments or struggles. Sometimes, the greatest gift you can give a person is to truly see and accept their experience.

Shattering Your Connections

Sometimes it can feel like giving empathy is too hard. Here we'll address some challenges and how to find your way around them. We focus on two of the biggest issues: unwanted problem solving and missing the cues that signal someone needs support.

Don't Problem Solve

Problem solving is one of your advisor's most powerful abilities, but in your relationships, it's the action that's likely to get you in trouble. People hate being solved.

If you are driving alone on a deserted road and your car makes funny noises, you can use your advisor to problem solve. *Is the car overheating? Should I keep driving? Can I call someone to come and get me?* You'll soon work out something to fix the problem. The car is physical, so problem solving works.

Now, if you make this same move in your relationships, you'll often experience disconnection. Someone close to you is moody, acts emotionally or selfishly, or expresses themselves poorly. Do you bring your advisor to the situation by problem solving? Do you "help" the person by telling them what ideas you have? Or quiz them on what's wrong? Do you tell them you have the solution? None of these will help; it's time to rest your advisor.

A person is more like a beautiful old oak tree than a car. You don't straighten up a big old tree. You merely sit under its shade or enjoy looking at its beauty. As you do, you'll see the weathered trunk and appreciate the struggle of storms it has endured. People are the same; try to appreciate their strengths and recognize and accept their emotion.

Don't Overlook Their Cues

Imagine a tired and irritable four-year-old. They say, "I wanted my sandwich cut in triangles, not quarters. I hate you." Then they throw themselves on the floor and have a tantrum. In these moments, you probably realize that their temper isn't really about the sandwich. The child doesn't need you to problem solve or explain. The tantrum is a cue for emotional help. If you know this, you'll soothe them, communicate love, and keep them safe while their big feelings rampage inside.

Adults signal for a loved one's attention too, but it is harder to see. Ask yourself, when you are stressed, overwhelmed, or emotional, do you usually come straight out and talk to your close connections, or do you sometimes send indirect messages? Maybe you get irritable, pick a fight, or go quiet. When someone you love makes an emotional statement, first consider that it might be a bid for your support. You might hear: "Would it hurt you to help me with the housework for once?" But what they are really saying is: "I feel undervalued. Do you care about me?" Consider an emotionally laden request from someone close to you as a time to try the two-step empathy process above.

Maintaining Self-Connection

There will be times when empathy is challenging, because you feel that someone has wronged you or empathy is too much effort. Your closest connections can often seem like the toughest part of your life. What can you do in these instances? It may seem paradoxical, but the first thing you need to do is connect with your own values and emotional reactions, rather than focusing exclusively on what the other person wants.

Choose Value First

What impedes connection, friendship, or love? This question might provoke many responses, including emotions like sadness, anxiety, hurt, or shame. Most often, what gets in the way is vulnerability and fear. Connection requires you to let your guard down, be open, and allow vulnerability to be in your life. It requires you to be undefended.

Your culture, learning, and history can make this difficult. If someone has shamed or hurt you, you may doubt the possibility of ever finding trust and connection. If you are socially anxious, you may feel you don't have good social skills. When these doubts overwhelm you, your advisor will turn *friendship* into *risk*. Ask yourself, if you keep others away, what will be the price that you will pay? Then, step into your value, listen to what your heart longs for, and follow your heart.

Don't Take Everything Personally

Sometimes loved ones can be irritable, impatient, or upset, and it isn't their fault or yours. Practice the empathy steps above. As you do, be aware of your emotional triggers. If what the other person is saying brings stress or intense emotions, you may not be able to provide them with empathy and you may not even be able to listen. If this happens, separate yourself for a time, as best you can. Try not to push back on your loved one. Let them know you need to come back to them by making an offer. For example, you might say, "I'm sorry, this is difficult for me to hear at the moment. Can we talk tomorrow? I just need some time." Buy time to consider what you feel and value in the relationship. Keep your commitment and follow through on whatever offer you've made.

Choose Your Connection Over Being Right

Another person might upset you and trigger defensiveness. You'll think things like, *They are in the wrong. They should hear my opinion. What about my views?* You'll feel the urge to fight to be right. This is a fight that many advisors love— winning an argument is powerfully reinforcing, but it can destroy relationships. Trying to win means you put empathy to the side, and you attack and defend with your words. Your relationship will be the cost. You do have a choice. Ask yourself, do you want to be right, or do you want to connect? If it is the latter, be willing to pause, give yourself time if you need it, and then practice empathy first. Do you care enough about this person to put being right aside?

Learn to Let Go

Finally, remember that even if you are skillful in your relationships, you may not resolve some relationship problems. Do people close to you often hurt you? Consider that a red flag. Those relationships may need re-evaluating. If you try practicing empathy first and you feel abused or trampled on, listen to your hurt. It may be time to put your self-care first. Return to the basic abilities, notic- ing-inside and noticing-outside, and putting your value of self-care in place. If you always feel like you are putting the other person first, or feel unsafe, it may be time to get professional help. Some people will manipulate your empathy to use you. Being kind, empathetic, and respectful is a strength. Don't let others turn it into a weakness and use it to abuse or dominate you.

....

Practicing Stronger Connections

Below are the steps for enhancing your close relationships. Try to use warm empathy first, and leave your advisor for later. Become aware of your attempts to problem solve other people and rebalance by perspective taking and sharing value. Also, remember, you have needs too, so valuing others must be in balance with caring for yourself.

Bringing more love and friendship into your life

Connection is your lifeline to well-being.

Two-step practice: Warm empathy, then cognitive empathy.

| *Perspective take.* | *Put shared value first.* | *Practice letting things go.* |

Unhelpful attempts to fix others: Problem-solving other people, missing their cues, needing to be right, taking things personally.

Unhelpful sacrifice to others: Losing contact with self-value and self-care, letting others treat you poorly.

Chapter 12

MANAGING DIFFICULTIES WITH OTHERS

If you want to master a difficult social situation, focus on effective strategies, not feel-good strategies. Showing people you are "right," criticizing them, and embarrassing them can make you feel good, but also converts potential allies into enemies.

"Hell is other people." That's a famous quote from Jean-Paul Sartre's play *No Exit*,[1] but he wasn't referring to all people; he meant hell was selfish, sadistic, or immoral people. You know the kind: they're often referred to as difficult. Louise can relate; here's her story.

I often wondered whether I was a magnet for conflict. In one of my workplaces, a male arrived every day in his navy-blue suit, carrying his 1960s briefcase, and giving the appearance of a mild-mannered, polite guy. Then he sabotaged all the women in the workplace. He threw things, lied about data, and collected evidence against staff members. The women complained, but senior men just didn't care: "It's a witch hunt," they said. The personal toll was immense: I lost sleep, ruined my family life, and eventually, exhausted, I resigned. In another workplace, my female boss would pit one employee against another. One day she told me I needed to purchase a stock item; later that same day, she told a colleague she'd fire me for purchasing it.

Louise did not know how to deal with these challenges. Many of us don't. This chapter can help you change that.

No matter whether you thrive on social interaction or consider yourself an introvert, you'll come across difficulties with other people. They'll be in your workplaces, community, and, sadly, sometimes in your family. It's likely that nobody trained you to manage difficulties with others. We'll help you identify what is going on and give you a new way to manage conflict.

Why Do We Blame Ourselves?

Let's return to Sartre's play, because it nicely illustrates the power of difficulties with others in our lives. The play centers on three unlikable characters: Garcin, Inez, and Estelle. All three have reprehensible histories. Garcin was a coward and unfaithful to his wife; Inez psychologically tortured a woman and pushed her to commit suicide, and Estelle threw her child off a hotel balcony and into the sea. All three characters die and end up in hell together. This hell is portrayed as being trapped in a windowless room with no exit. Each character is forced for all of eternity to see themselves through the disapproving eyes of the other two. Disapproval *is* hell for each of them, just as it is for all of us.

Consider your workplace or social setting, where someone seems to always be criticizing or bullying you. If they're judging you, you'll feel bad and probably think it's your fault, at least for a short time. It's relatively automatic. We are a group species and emotions like guilt or shame kick in quickly when there is social stress. These feelings are not wrong; they help you monitor your social status and get back into the group, and they probably worked well when humans lived in small hunter-gatherer villages. Workplaces don't have the same reciprocity of small villages, though: they have wolves. All this means that if someone is judging you harshly, you might spend a bit of time blaming yourself. You can't really protect yourself entirely from hurt—you might feel hurt even when you *know* their judgment is wrong, and even if you have high self-esteem and supportive friends.[2]

The judgment or bullying can trigger a downward spiral too. The cycle can look like this: they criticize you—you feel hurt and angry—you judge and confront them—and that prompts them to criticize you even more. If you're stuck in this cycle, it's time to change.

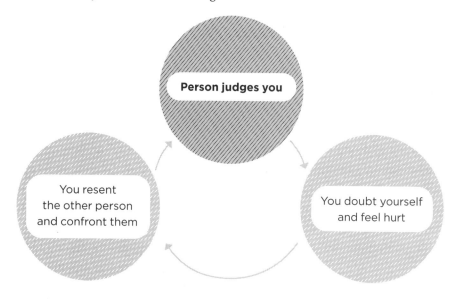

Know What Kind of Difficulty You Face

Your first step in managing conflict is to know the difficulty you face. Be honest with yourself. Is the problem with them, or is it with you? Is the person actually difficult? Remember, other people have their own needs, and they won't always have your best interests in mind. Is there conflict because the other person's needs are different from yours? Accept that people will put their needs first sometimes. Try to find the right balance of give and take.

If you've tried to balance your and their needs and the conflict persists, then you might be facing a difficult person. The data on difficulties with others suggests it is pervasive in our lives.[3] It's hard to know what behaviors denote a *difficult* person. It isn't always easy to recognize when people have pushed beyond acceptable boundaries, by acting selfishly or aggressively or being manipulative. Here are some clues to look for.

Selfish Behavior

Selfishness is present whenever another person consistently disregards what you want or need. It's always their way. They'll do things like take advantage of you, put you down, dominate you to achieve their goals, or always put their interests ahead of yours.

Aggressive Behavior

Aggressive behavior occurs when someone tries to harm you or hurt your feelings repeatedly (i.e., it is not a one-off). Aggression can be subtle, so it's worth talking about the four types of aggression.

Direct aggression is obvious to everybody. The person physically or verbally attacks you, makes fun of you, insults you, or puts you down because of your religion, gender, race, or other characteristics.

Passive aggression involves somebody trying to hurt you indirectly instead of openly addressing an issue with you. Examples include backhanded compliments, secretly undermining your efforts, playing the victim, refusing to communicate with you, sulking, and using sarcasm.

Social aggression involves people gossiping behind your back and creating alliances against you.

Cyber aggression involves attempts to hurt you through any type of social media, such as chats, forums, websites, and emails. The internet has increased the opportunity for people to attack, hate, and criticize. This includes passive-aggressive behavior like trolling, which can include constantly writing emotionally laden comments designed to manipulate perceptions, expressing "concern" that you are wrong, or disagreeing with anything you post.

Manipulative Behavior

Manipulative behavior takes the form of a manipulator blaming others, twisting the truth, aligning people against you, and changing events in their favor and at your expense. These behaviors can be tough to spot because manipulative people often appear charming. However, they gaslight you by rewriting events and creating confusion about what happened. They can act defensively by turning themselves into the victim. They can make you feel like it's all your fault. You might know people who act manipulatively as *narcissists*. They are not uncommon in families and workplaces.[4]

....

Identify Your Typical Strategy

We all have default ways we try to handle difficulties with others. It's good to know yours. Once you recognize your typical conflict strategy, you are in a better position to evaluate whether it is working. There are potentially an infinite number of strategies you could use, but there is a simple way to classify every possible response into one of four categories, based on whether you are supporting the person's needs, discouraging the person's behavior, doing both, or doing neither. Let's apply this thinking to a real issue. Think of some conflict you had with a difficult person recently. Then read through the following strategies and see whether you overuse one.

FOUR STRATEGIES TO EXPLORE, WHEN DEALING WITH A DIFFICULT SOCIAL SITUATION.

IGNORE OR ESCAPE.

STAND UP FOR YOURSELF.

BE SUPPORTIVE.

BE SUPPORTIVE AND STAND UP FOR YOURSELF.

Strategy 1: Ignore or Escape

This strategy includes pretending the incident did not occur, leaving, or avoiding the situation. Sometimes this strategy is workable, especially when other strategies make things worse. Sometimes the best response is to not respond, let time pass, and be patient. However, make sure you consider other strategies before you conclude doing nothing or escaping is your only move.

Strategy 2: Stand Up for Yourself

This strategy involves being assertive and focuses on reducing unwanted behavior. You might use this strategy to set firm boundaries with a person to prevent the behavior from reoccurring. It is also useful when you don't want to be friends with the person.

When seeking to discourage unhelpful behavior by standing up for yourself, a graded approach is often best. Start with mild discouragement and work your way up to firmer discouragement only if the person is unresponsive. For example, if someone keeps dumping work on you at the last minute, and you suspect they are doing it to hurt you, you might initially be polite and clear: "Please give me the work within realistic time lines." If the behavior continues, you can then increase your assertiveness: "It's unhelpful to give me this work so close to the deadline. Please provide me with more notice." If their behavior still doesn't change, you might need to become firmer: "It's inappropriate to continue giving me work at the last minute. If you can't give me the work earlier, I'll have to discuss it with management." When you are under pressure, you might be tempted to use the strongest strategy first, but be careful. These strategies often have consequences, such as making the person a permanent enemy. Use the minimum force necessary to influence the other person.

Strategy 3: Be Supportive

This strategy is a little less obvious and involves selectively reinforcing the kind of behavior you want from the other person, hoping it will replace the behavior you don't want. You might validate the person's struggle, say something positive, or reinforce the actions you like. In the deadline example above, you might say something like, "Last week I really appreciated you giving me the work with a full week's notice. It was thoughtful. Thank you. I'm wondering if I can work with you moving forward to continue achieving this every week?"

Strategy 4: Be Supportive and Stand Up for Yourself

With this strategy, you are being supportive, but firm and assertive. In the deadline example, you might say, "Last week I really appreciated you giving me the work with a full week's notice. It was thoughtful. Thank you. However, some weeks I've had less notice, and this increases my work pressure. Moving forward I would appreciate a full week's notice." This may seem like it is always the best strategy, but it can be ineffective in some contexts. For example, sometimes managers are taught to sandwich negative feedback inside positive feedback. They might say something like, "I just want to say how happy I have been with your work. However, this recent job was substandard. You will need to improve. But I still love your work."

This strategy is so familiar to some employees that they have taken to calling it a "shit sandwich," since what is in the middle is so bad. They also start to cringe every time their manager says something positive because they know that something negative is coming. The point is, you never want to use any strategy in a rigid and stereotyped way. Flexibility is the key.

Do you default to any of the four strategies across multiple situations? For example, are you always resolving conflict by trying to be agreeable (strategy 3), or by arguing and seeking to dominate (strategy 2)? Perhaps you avoid conflict at all costs (strategy 1)? Maybe you are *always* supporting helpful and discouraging unhelpful actions (strategy 4); even this can become a problem when occasionally letting things go (strategy 1) might be best. No strategy works every time. The key is to notice your default strategy, and if it is not working, to pause and try something else.

....

How to Try a New Strategy

Trying a new strategy requires two things: pausing and choosing valued action.

Pause

If you have decided you want to try a new strategy, you will need to use your pause abilities to disrupt your old strategy. Notice your urge to rapidly respond in your typical style. Slow down and breathe. What does the urge feel like in your body? Notice your feet on the ground.

When facing conflict, you might find yourself in fight-or-flight mode, feeling vulnerable and tipped toward stress. Your body and mind become charged with energy, seeking a way out. If this happens, you might respond too quickly. You sense an urgency to fire off that email or directly confront the person. Your body and brain are on alert, saying, "Fight back. Get away. Now. Do something!" This is the time to pause.

You usually have more time to respond than you think. Slow down and get a complete and accurate assessment of the situation. The more you take in and consider, the better your response.

During this pause, remind yourself what you value. How do you want to act during this conflict? Calm, dignified, strong, assertive, effective? What do you want to accomplish? What would be an ideal outcome here?

You might be tempted to do something that *feels* good but makes things worse. For example, if someone has angered you, you fire off an email attacking them. Or you might confront them in front of others, making them feel foolish and put in their place. This may make you feel good and even reduce their unwanted behavior for a short time. However, it may also make them feel embarrassed. Beware of moral and public attacks. The person may give in, but they won't forget. They may resent you, secretly undermine you, and turn people against you. If you are tempted to use an unhelpful feel-good strategy, return to the pause ability above.

> Is your conflict strategy about feeling good,
> or being effective?

Choose Valued Action

Now that you have learned to pause, you have opened up space to try something new. The next question is, what will this new strategy or behavior be?

No single strategy always works in every situation with every person. People may tell you to be assertive, but what if that strategy encourages the other person to attack you? People may tell you to discuss your feelings, but what if the person uses your feelings against you to hurt you? You don't need to rigidly follow social rules; you need to find social strategies that work for you, in your situation. It's time for discovery.

Step 1. Explore the Four Strategies

The first step is to deliberately consider a wide range of options, even ones your advisor says have no chance of working. Let's do that now. Think of a difficult situation and imagine using each of these strategies with the person.

- » Imagine trying to ignore or escape the situation.
- » Imagine standing up for yourself.
- » Imagine being supportive and reinforcing their positive behavior.
- » Imagine being supportive and standing up for yourself.

Step 2. Take One Bold Step

Now that you have considered several strategies, decide which one you are willing to try. Are you willing to feel distress to try this strategy? If your answer is yes, then try it. If your answer is no, then seek another strategy or find a less distressing way to implement your preferred strategy.

Step 3. Stay Open to Feedback

Did the strategy work? Did you get the outcome you wanted? If not, you may need to return to step 1 and try something else.

There are two concrete ways to increase the chance of your strategy working. First, start with trust, where possible. Assume that the other person can improve their behavior. Give people the benefit of the doubt, and they will often surprise you. Second, seek to create a shared narrative. Rather than attacking the person, see if you can find common ground. Ask yourself, *What do we both want?* Then ask, *How can we work together to get it?*

Step 4. Turn Conflict into Support

The four strategies above are useful when seeking to resolve a specific conflict. Sometimes you can make a deeper change with the person and transform your relationship so that it is mutually supportive rather than conflictual. We do this by focusing on their and your values.

Do you know what your person values? Can you take their perspective and see what matters to them? Taking the perspective of another person can be painful. You may be tempted to just block them out. But the better you understand their position, the more prepared you are to respond effectively. You can assume that the other person is motivated by one of three needs:[5]

To feel in control

To feel competent

To feel valued and accepted as a person

For example, say a colleague is constantly and unfairly criticizing your work. You might ask yourself, what is motivating them? Are they criticizing you because they need to feel in control and powerful? Or are they threatened by your skill and need to feel competent around you? Try to guess what they need. Then, try turning conflict into alliance by experimenting with different ways to support their needs. Although this feels counterintuitive and probably goes against your initial impulse, this approach of meeting their underlying needs can lead to more of the behavior you desire from them.

Let's look at an example. Say you suspect your difficult person is motivated to feel more competent. Your strategy would then be to meet that competency need by validating their skill when they do something well. Then, watch what happens next. Do they seem pleased or content? Do they stop criticizing you?

If yes, then you may have guessed their motive. If no, then you can try another strategy.

This approach is about trying something out and monitoring the consequences. We are not suggesting you should always use these kinds of supportive, need-fulfillment strategies, but if you can do it without inhibiting your own needs, you might give it a try.

What If Nothing Works?

If you reach a point where all strategies repeatedly fail, then the solution may be to leave or escape. Break the cycle. Unfortunately, you'll face situations where you are forced to interact with a difficult person and cannot get away. It might be in your workplace, in social circles, in the community, and sometimes even in your family.

A cautionary note is essential: If you are in a relationship with someone who leaves you feeling unsafe, abused, or in danger, don't manage this difficult person alone. Seek support first. The strategies we discuss in this book help with difficulties with other people, such as work colleagues, but an abusive partner or similar high-risk situation is altogether different. Seek help. Remind yourself that getting help is not a weakness but a strength.

Practicing New Ways to Manage Difficulty

When difficulties with others present themselves, practice the strategies that are summarized below. Try to explore multiple actions and stay open to feedback on how each attempt works.

Managing difficulties with others

Pause and consider value for you and the relationship.

Explore multiple strategies, try something new, stay open to feedback, seek help.

Try actions that flip conflict to connection.

Being overly agreeable:
Not considering your needs, giving in to the other's needs, not having limits or boundaries.

Being overly aggressive:
Trying to convice, argue, be aggressive, or attack the other.

Chapter 13

ACTIVE HOPE AS THE WORLD CHANGES

We cannot turn away from this catastrophe because there is no "away" to turn toward. There is no escaping this Earth. When we acknowledge the crisis, we become able to take bold steps and create hope.

I t would be negligent for a book on change to ignore the biggest changes facing all of us. Right now, the world faces unprecedented change at every level: individual, social, political, economic, and environmental. Throughout this book, we have encouraged you to be open to your pain and to change. You have seen that opening up creates a path toward hope, while avoidance increases your struggle and despair. Humans excel at problem solving, but we can't solve what we refuse to see. It's time to lean in, not turn away from our changing world.

We write the following based on science: The international community of scientists agrees the planet is warming rapidly, and faster than their data predictions.[1] Animal and plant species are facing the sixth mass extinction. Oceans are acidifying. Icecaps are melting. These changes will bring extreme weather events, water shortages, fires, desertification, failed crops, and food shortages. Historically, changes like this bring war and conflict too. Pause to consider just one of these changes: The United Nations has predicted that two-thirds of the population will face water shortages by 2025.[2] Let that last data point sink in, notice the magnitude of it, and pay attention to the year. It makes your gut sink, doesn't it? But if we ignore the data, we hurt the health and well-being of ourselves, future generations, and all living things. The climate crisis is bearing down on us.

The world convulses with unwanted change. In 2020, a pandemic brought the world to its knees. People lost loved ones, faced long-term illness, unemployment, economic hardship, and lockdowns that would have been unimaginable just one year prior. We watched as distance shut off loved ones whom we longed to hug again. Voids opened in our lives. The borders of countries closed. We sealed elder care and hospital ICU doors, even as our loved ones passed away inside. We didn't see it coming, and as change often does, it left us no choice but to adapt.

The greatest challenges in modern human history are here. Now.

This brief closing chapter will show you how to use your DNA-V abilities to build active hope, find purpose, and face these struggles. Each reader will stand in a different place in terms of their views, knowledge, capacity, and willingness to act. Difference is okay. There is no shame in being a person who acts by quietly growing vegetables or a person who acts with a loud public voice. The only shame is not acting. We must honestly see the crisis, consider what we can all do, and help change our world. We don't provide specific advice here, like telling you to stop flying or driving; those details are for other experts. Here we show how your DNA-V abilities, a system based on behavioral science, can help you face a crisis and bring active hope. You can help your children, your family, and our world. It's up to you and us. Facing this change is a painful process, but it is our only chance at survival.

....

Use Your Noticer's Strength to See Our Pain

Negative emotions are not like negative external threats. When you touch a hot stove, you pull away. Avoidance helps. Many cultures have norms that follow the same logic for negative emotions—if it hurts, make it stop, block it out, shut it down, and pull away from the source of pain. But research using acceptance and commitment therapy has repeatedly shown that the reverse is the rule for emotional pain.[3] When you avoid emotional pain, like sadness, anxiety, and anger, it doesn't go away; it simmers and often grows. And, when you're avoiding the emotional pain of an undeniable crisis, you're playing the violin while the *Titanic* sinks. It can't end well.

There is another way. Use your noticer ability to allow your emotions instead of blocking them. Turn your pain into purpose. If we all turn away from the crisis, we will make the pain worse. We will spend all our time arguing, denying, and fighting each other instead of the problem. If instead we stay open to the shared pain, we can recognize we are in this together. Solidarity brings hope. Not listening allows us to turn away from suffering in the short term, but the problem won't disappear. Be willing to listen. We know the pain is terrible; it may bring tears to your eyes or make your heart ache, *and* it puts you in a position to do something.

Use Your Advisor's Vision

In the introductory chapter, we listed five reasons that people resist change. We come back to this now and show how your advisor behaves in crisis.

First, unaware or untrained, your advisor will guide you away from immediate distress. Your advisor might suggest you turn away from the fear and uncertainty and keep living the same lifestyle, pretending nothing is changing. You might stop watching the news in favor of the comfort of a sitcom, or worse, find comfort inside social media, or anti-science echo chambers. Human civilizations have collapsed before because of their inability to change. Our civilization is not immune.

Second, your advisor might suggest you turn away because you have a lowered sense of competence. For example, you might say to yourself, *I'm just one person. What can I do? The governments need to fix it.* It's easy for our advisor to lose sight of the power of one person leading a group change. Rosa Parks, for example, was just one Black American woman who refused to surrender her seat to a white male, but she became a catalyst for the American civil rights movement.

Third, we don't like to feel controlled. For example, when advocacy groups suggest you make changes, like taking public transport, stop eating meat, or wear a mask, your advisor can get rigid and demand that others have no right to tell you how to live. We may rebel against public health policies so that we *feel* in control, even as we lose control of our planet.

Fourth, your advisor will tell you it's too hard, just too much effort. Changing your behavior from being a polluter to a considerate consumer can be hard, but turning away will be catastrophic in the long run.

Finally, the hardest of all is that your advisor tells you that your negative predictions are correct. Rome is burning; it's too late. You might think it's hopeless.

Instead of using your advisor in habitual ways, use it to find ways out of this dilemma. When you feel hopeless, remind yourself that your advisor is poor at predicting the future. Look at it like this: if you think back just a few years, what did you think 2022 would be like? Would you have predicted a pandemic in 2004 when Facebook launched, in 2007 when the final Harry Potter book was released, or in 2008 when the first Black president was elected in the United States? Imagine if we had tapped you on the shoulder and asked your advisor to predict. Do you think your advisor would have predicted that governments would lock people down to prevent death? Or that racial inequality would seem further away? Or that world leaders would *still* argue over climate science while the world got noticeably hotter? Probably not. We have shown that your advisor's job is to predict threats and focus on the negative. If you listened to your advisor right now, your predictions might be that we can't stop this boat from sinking. You will notice powerful emotions, maybe despair, rage, or frustration. And your actions may be to give up. To live like there is no tomorrow—to hell with it—just dance. But your advisor's incorrect predictions are the very reason to hope. Its negative predictions can be wrong.

The advisor is still the most powerful problem-solving machine ever, if you use it. Right now, visionary people worldwide are acknowledging their pain and using their advisor superpower to find solutions. We can fix many issues, but only if we look at the problem and embrace new technology.[4] In many cases, the technology we need has already been invented.[5] We can harness the oceans to create seaweed forests that draw down carbon from the atmosphere. The technology that we love so much can run on renewable energy and allow us to keep fossil fuels in the ground while we still use cars and computers. Drones are available that can plant millions of trees and reforest at a rapid rate. Economists have provided new economic paradigms, such as the "donut economy," that create equality and community.[6] There are so many examples. You see, the human advisor is visionary if you turn it to finding solutions, not shutting off and avoiding. We are all needed to save our world. There is hope only in collective action. In inaction, there is only despair.

Step into Your Discoverer with New Action

When you come face to face with the crisis, you may retreat to the safe and familiar. Remember that habit zone? Turn off the news and do something that brings you comfort. It's hard to change and open up to new actions that cause discomfort. You might get reactive; maybe you want to stop reading this chapter because it is confronting. You might shut down, turn off, and turn away. But know this: your discoverer is a great ally when facing the struggles around you.

Discovery is where new actions can bring hope. Be curious, explore, step into uncertainty, and take the smallest of steps. That is a start—small, bold steps. Billions of people taking small actions is *a lot of action*. Science shows the benefits of small steps. For example, giving to others helps people recover from depression; it helps the giver as much as the receiver.[7] Volunteering helps the charity and builds purpose in the volunteer.[8] The first step you take can be effortful, but you will gain momentum.

You will become more hopeful when you take action.[9] For the most significant issues like our planet's health, take any step, no matter how small. Maybe you will choose to write to your politicians, grow plants, fly carbon neutral, or have less meat a few days a week. We know slight changes won't by themselves halt climate change—we are way beyond recycling as a means to save the planet—but these steps are to start *you* on the process. Why does that matter? Behavioral science shows us that first steps lead to more steps.[10] You just have to start.

Strength in Numbers

The power of humanity lies in our ability to function, not as selfish individuals but as like-minded groups.[11] Families cooperate and become communities. Communities link to countries and then to humanity. All that power of cooperative groups, small to large, remains today.

For example, a small teenage girl from Sweden sitting outside parliament protesting climate inaction started a global movement of school children striking for climate action. You no doubt know of Greta Thunberg and her call to action that captured the hearts and minds of millions of young activists worldwide. Do remember, though, that she was just one small person at the start. She was willing to face opposition from her parents and teachers and take valued action.

She developed a small group; that group then developed into thousands of small groups. The school strikes for climate action prompted four million students to protest over four days in September 2019[12] and millions more over the ensuing years. The steps are there—take a small action and connect with a group.

There are many groups of all kinds working toward active hope. There is everything from radical activists to conservative groups.[13] What matters is knowing that like-minded people working at the grassroots level create movements. A small group of eight students began a class action suit against their government, demanding duty of care be given to children and their future.[14] There are many examples like this worldwide. The Intergovernmental Panel on Climate Change was established with 195 governments all working together to assess and act.[15] People can come together and create power through numbers and that can influence governments. Groups of ordinary people can influence capital investment. The International Monetary Fund has announced that fossil fuels will likely become stranded assets and they argue that we care for the natural world with new economic policies. You are not small when you join with others to take economic action. We don't know what might happen if small investments and savings were shifted toward renewables. We do know grassroots groups are waking up to the power that is magnified inside like-minded group collaborations. You can create hope and strength in your small groups.

....

Each Day, Value and Hope

We began this book talking of longing and change. We called on you to open up to your heart's deepest longings for your life. To open up to the purpose and value that you hold. We end the book in the same way. We know that the changes facing the world can feel crushing. Think about the power you have if you open your heart to your values, allow the pain, and refuse to look away. Turn the pain of world change into your passion and power. No matter what level of change you plan, know that your heartfelt efforts will matter. Every valued action, no matter how small, can change the world.

What if
The world does end
Will end
Has ended
And it's already too late

But that's okay
Because the old world was never yours
It was made by those who came before you
When you were just a whisper
Of their imagination
On the edge of a dream
That they could never quite recall
When they awoke

And you will mold the new world
Between your fingers
Like a potter with clay
And it will be messy
And you will get dirty
And it will spin and collapse

And then, if you are gentle
And patient
And you don't give up
It will rise again
And take shape
In your hands

Into something that's beautiful
Something that's yours
That is exactly as amazing,
No, even more so
Than you could possibly imagine?

— Lisa Coyne, "Poem at the End of the World"[16]

Endnotes

Introduction

1   L. L. Hayes and J. Ciarrochi, *The Thriving Adolescent: Using Acceptance and Commitment Therapy and Positive Psychology to Help Teens Manage Emotions, Achieve Goals, and Build Connection* (Oakland, CA: New Harbinger, 2015).

2   L. N. Landy, R. L. Schneider, and J. J. Arch, "Acceptance and Commitment Therapy for the Treatment of Anxiety Disorders: A Concise Review," *Current Opinion in Psychology* 2 (2015): 70–74.

E. B. Lee, W. An, M. E. Levin, and M. P. Twohig, "An Initial Meta-Analysis of Acceptance and Commitment Therapy for Treating Substance Use Disorders," *Drug Alcohol Dependence* 155 (2015): 1–7.

M. E. Levin, M. J. Hildebrandt, J. Lillis, and S. C. Hayes, "The Impact of Treatment Components Suggested by the Psychological Flexibility Model: A Meta-Analysis of Laboratory-Based Component Studies," *Behavior Therapy* 43 (2012): 741–756.

S. C. Hayes, K. D. Strosahl, and K. G. Wilson, *Acceptance and Commitment Therapy, Second Edition: The Process and Practice of Mindful Change* (New York: Guilford Press, 2016).

3   J. Ciarrochi, P. W. B. Atkins, L. L. Hayes, B. K. Sahdra, and P. Parker, "Contextual Positive Psychology: Policy Recommendations for Implementing Positive Psychology into Schools," *Frontiers in Psychology* 7 (2016): 1561.

T. B. Kashdan and J. Ciarrochi, *Mindfulness, Acceptance, and Positive Psychology: The Seven Foundations of Well-Being* (Oakland, CA: Context Press, 2013).

4   J. Ciarrochi, S. Hayes, L. Hayes, B. Sahdra, M. Ferrari, K. Yap, S. Hofmann (in press), "From Package to Process: An Evidence-Based Approach to Processes of Change in Psychotherapy," in S. Hofmann (ed.), *Comprehensive Clinical Psychology: Foundations*. Elsevier.

5   L. O. Fjorback, M. Arendt, E. Ornbøl, P. Fink, and H. Walach, "Mindfulness-Based Stress Reduction and Mindfulness-Based Cognitive Therapy: A Systematic Review of Randomized Controlled Trials," *Acta Psychiatrica Scandinavica* 124 (2011): 102–119.

6 R. M. Ryan and E. L. Deci, *Self-Determination Theory: Basic Psychological Needs in Motivation, Development, and Wellness* (New York: Guilford Press, 2017).

7 M. D. Ainsworth, M. Blehar, E. Waters, and S. Wall, *Patterns of Attachment: A Psychological Study of the Strange Situation* (Hillsdale, NJ: Erlbaum, 1978).

8 S. C. Hayes, S. G. Hofmann, and J. Ciarrochi, "A Process-Based Approach to Psychological Diagnosis and Treatment: The Conceptual and Treatment Utility of an Extended Evolutionary Meta Model," *Clinical Psychology Review* 82 (2020): 101908.

Chapter 1

1 G. Basarkod, B. K. Sahdra, N. Hooper, and J. Ciarrochi, *The Six Ways to Well-Being (6W-WeB): Assessing the Frequency of and Motivation for Six Behaviours Linked to Well-Being*, PsyArXiv (September 30, 2019), doi:10.31234/osf.io/jtcng.

2 G. L. Cohen and D. K. Sherman, "The Psychology of Change: Self-Affirmation and Social Psychological Intervention," *Annual Review of Psychology* 65 (2014): 333–371.

3 J. A. Chase, et al., "Values Are Not Just Goals: Online ACT-Based Values Training Adds to Goal Setting in Improving Undergraduate College Student Performance," *Journal of Contextual Behavioral Science* 2 (2013): 79–84.

4 G. L. Cohen, J. Garcia, N. Apfel, and A. Master, "Reducing the Racial Achievement Gap: A Social-Psychological Intervention," *Science* 313 (2006): 1307–1310.

5 B. M. Smith, et al., "The Influence of a Personal Values Intervention on Cold Pressor-Induced Distress Tolerance," *Behavior Modification* 43 (2019): 688–710.

6 E. R. Hebert, M. K. Flynn, K. G. Wilson, and K. K. Kellum, "Values Intervention as an Establishing Operation for Approach in the Presence of Aversive Stimuli," *Journal of Contextual Behavioral Science* 20 (2021): 144–154.

Chapter 2

1 N. Torneke, *Learning RFT: An Introduction to Relational Frame Theory and Its Clinical Application* (Oakland, CA: New Harbinger Publications, 2010).

2 Torneke, *Learning RFT*.

3 R. F. Baumeister, E. Bratslavsky, C. Finkenauer, and K. D. Vohs, "Bad Is Stronger Than Good," *Review of General Psychology* 5 (2001): 323–370.

4 Torneke, *Learning RFT*.

5 Baumeister, *Bad Is Stronger Than Good*.

6 R. Brockman, J. Ciarrochi, P. Parker, and T. Kashdan, "Emotion Regulation Strategies in Daily Life: Mindfulness, Cognitive Reappraisal and Emotion Suppression," *Cognitive Behaviour Therapy* 46 (2017): 91–113.

7 S. C. Hayes, K. G. Wilson, E. V. Gifford, V. M. Follette, and K. Strosahl, "Experiential Avoidance and Behavioral Disorders: A Functional Dimensional Approach to Diagnosis and Treatment," *Journal of Clinical and Consulting Psychology* 64 (1996): 1152–1168.

8 D. A. Assaz, B. Roche, J. W. Kanter, and C. K. B. Oshiro, "Cognitive Defusion in Acceptance and Commitment Therapy: What Are the Basic Processes of Change?" *Psychological Record* 68 (2018): 405–418.

Chapter 3

1 A. Ortony, G. Clore, and A. Collins, *The Cognitive Structure of Emotion* (Cambridge, UK: Cambridge University Press, 1988).

B. L. Fredrickson and M. F. Losada, "Positive Affect and the Complex Dynamics of Human Flourishing," *American Psychologist* 60 (2005): 678–686.

2 T. B. Kashdan, V. Barrios, J. P. Forsyth, and M. F. Steger, "Experiential Avoidance as a Generalized Psychological Vulnerability: Comparisons with Coping and Emotion Regulation Strategies," *Behaviour Research and Therapy* 44 (2006): 1301–1320.

T. B. Kashdan, et al., "A Contextual Approach to Experiential Avoidance and Social Anxiety: Evidence from an Experimental Interaction and Daily Interactions of People with Social Anxiety Disorder," *Emotion* 14 (2014): 769–781.

3 P. Cuijpers, E. Karyotaki, L. de Wit, and D. D. Ebert, "The Effects of Fifteen Evidence-Supported Therapies for Adult Depression: A Meta-Analytic Review," *Psychotherapy Research* 30 (2020): 279–293.

4 B. Brown, *Daring Greatly: How the Courage to Be Vulnerable Transforms the Way We Live, Love, Parent, and Lead* (New York: Penguin, 2015).

5 Cuijpers, "The Effects of Fifteen Evidence-Supported Therapies for Adult Depression."

Brown, *Daring Greatly.*

6 K. Sanada, et al., "Effects of Mindfulness-Based Interventions on Salivary Cortisol in Healthy Adults: A Meta-Analytical Review," *Frontiers in Physiology* 7 (2016): 471.

L. O. Fjorback, M. Arendt, E. Ornbøl, P. Fink, and H. Walach, "Mindfulness-Based Stress Reduction and Mindfulness-Based Cognitive Therapy: A Systematic Review of Randomized Controlled Trials," *Acta Psychiatrica Scandinavica* 124 (2011): 102–119.

E. Malcoun, "Unpacking Mindfulness: Psychological Processes Underlying the Health Benefits of a Mindfulness-Based Stress Reduction Program" (PhD diss., Bryn Mawr College, 2008).

7 J. Ciarrochi, P. C. L. Heaven, and S. Supavadeeprasit, "The Link Between Emotion Identification Skills and Socio-Emotional Functioning in Early Adolescence: A 1-Year Longitudinal Study," *Journal of Adolescence* 31 (2008): 565–582.

J. B. Torre and M. D. Lieberman, "Putting Feelings into Words: Affect Labeling as Implicit Emotion Regulation," *Emotion Review* 10 (2018): 116–124.

8 Sanada, "Effects of Mindfulness-Based Interventions on Salivary Cortisol in Healthy Adults."

Fjorback, "Mindfulness-Based Stress Reduction and Mindfulness-Based Cognitive Therapy."

Malcoun, "Unpacking Mindfulness."

Chapter 4

1   A. Gopnik, et al., "Changes in Cognitive Flexibility and Hypothesis Search Across Human Life History from Childhood to Adolescence to Adulthood," *Proceedings of the National Academy of Sciences of the USA* 114 (2017): 7892–7899.

2   Gopnik, "Changes in Cognitive Flexibility."

3   T. P. German and M. A. Defeyter, "Immunity to Functional Fixedness in Young Children," *Psychonomic Bulletin & Review* 7 (2000): 707–712.

4   D. J. Plebanek and V. M. Sloutsky, "Costs of Selective Attention: When Children Notice What Adults Miss," *Psychological Science* 28 (2017): 723–732.

    V. M. Sloutsky and A. V. Fisher, "When Development and Learning Decrease Memory: Evidence Against Category-Based Induction in Children," *Psychological Science* 15 (2004): 553–558.

5   Gopnik, "Changes in Cognitive Flexibility."

6   S. McLoughlin, I. Tyndall, and A. Pereira, "Relational Operant Skills Training Increases Standardized Matrices Scores in Adolescents: A Stratified Active-Controlled Trial," *Journal of Behavioral Education* (2020), doi:10.1007/s10864-020-09399-x.

7   B.-Y. Li, Y. Wang, H.-D. Tang, and S.-D. Chen, "The Role of Cognitive Activity in Cognition Protection: From Bedside to Bench," *Translational Neurodegeneration* 6 (2017): 7.

8   E. L. Garland, et al., "Upward Spirals of Positive Emotions Counter Downward Spirals of Negativity: Insights from the Broaden-and-Build Theory and Affective Neuroscience on the Treatment of Emotion Dysfunctions and Deficits in Psychopathology," *Clinical Psychology Review* 30 (2010): 849–864.

Chapter 5

1   C. Lewis, N. P. Roberts, M. Andrew, E. Starling, and J. I. Bisson, "Psychological Therapies for Post-Traumatic Stress Disorder in Adults: Systematic Review and Meta-Analysis," *European Journal of Psychotraumatology* 11 (2020): 1729633.

2   J. Kolacz, et al., "Adversity History Predicts Self-Reported Autonomic Reactivity and Mental Health in US Residents During the COVID-19 Pandemic," *Frontiers in Psychiatry* 11 (2020): 577728.

B. A. Van der Kolk, *The Body Keeps the Score: Brain, Mind, and Body in the Healing of Trauma* (New York: Penguin, 2015).

3   S. W. Porges, "The Polyvagal Theory: New Insights into Adaptive Reactions of the Autonomic Nervous System," *Cleveland Clinic Journal of Medicine* 76 Suppl 2 (2009): S86-90.

4   Porges, "The Polyvagal Theory."

K. Roelofs, "Freeze for Action: Neurobiological Mechanisms in Animal and Human Freezing," *Philosophical Transactions of the Royal Society of London, Series B, Biological Sciences* 372 (2017).

5   C. Schiweck, D. Piette, D. Berckmans, S. Claes, and E. Vrieze, "Heart Rate and High Frequency Heart Rate Variability During Stress as Biomarker for Clinical Depression: A Systematic Review," *Psychological Medicine* 49 (2019): 200–211.

6   Schiweck, "Heart Rate and High Frequency Heart Rate Variability."

J. F. Thayer, F. Ahs, M. Fredrikson, J. J. Sollers III, and T. D. Wager, "A Meta-Analysis of Heart Rate Variability and Neuroimaging Studies: Implications for Heart Rate Variability as a Marker of Stress and Health," *Neuroscience & Biobehavioral Reviews* 36 (2012): 747–756.

I. Grossmann, B. K. Sahdra, and J. Ciarrochi, "A Heart and a Mind: Self-Distancing Facilitates the Association Between Heart Rate Variability and Wise Reasoning," *Frontiers in Behavioral Neuroscience* 10 (2016): 68.

B. K. Sahdra, J. Ciarrochi, and P. D. Parker, "High-Frequency Heart Rate Variability Linked to Affiliation with a New Group," *PLoS One* 10 (2015): e0129583.

L. R. Wulsin, P. S. Horn, J. L. Perry, J. M. Massaro, and R. B. D'Agostino, "Autonomic Imbalance as a Predictor of Metabolic Risks, Cardiovascular Disease, Diabetes, and Mortality," *Journal of Clinical Endocrinology and Metabolism* 100 (2015): 2443–2448.

7   Kolacz, "Adversity History Predicts Self-Reported Autonomic Reactivity."

8   C. Benjet, et al., "The Epidemiology of Traumatic Event Exposure World-wide: Results from the World Mental Health Survey Consortium," *Psychological Medicine* 46 (2016): 327–343.

9   H. Yaribeygi, Y. Panahi, H. Sahraei, T. P. Johnston, and A. Sahebkar, "The Impact of Stress on Body Function: A Review," *EXCLI Journal* 16 (2017): 1057–1072.

10 R. F. Krueger, B. M. Hicks, and M. McGue, "Altruism and Antisocial Behavior: Independent Tendencies, Unique Personality Correlates, Distinct Etiologies," *Psychological Science* 12 (2001): 397–402.

M. J. Poulin, et al., "Does a Helping Hand Mean a Heavy Heart? Helping Behavior and Well-Being Among Spouse Caregivers," *Psychology and Aging* 25 (2010): 108–117.

11 C. Schwartz, J. B. Meisenhelder, Y. Ma, and G. Reed, "Altruistic Social Interest Behaviors Are Associated with Better Mental Health," *Psychosomatic Medicine* 65 (2003): 778–785.

12 J. Ciarrochi, R. Harris, and A. Bailey, *The Weight Escape: Stop Fad Dieting, Start Losing Weight and Reshape Your Life Using Cutting-Edge Psychology* (London: Hachette UK, 2015).

J.-P. Chaput, et al., "Sleep Timing, Sleep Consistency, and Health in Adults: A Systematic Review," *Applied Physiology, Nutrition, and Metabolism* 45 (2020): S232–S247.

P. de Souto Barreto, Y. Rolland, B. Vellas, and M. Maltais, "Association of Long-term Exercise Training with Risk of Falls, Fractures, Hospitalizations, and Mortality in Older Adults: A Systematic Review and Meta-Analysis," *JAMA of Internal Medicine* 179 (2019): 394–405.

J. P. Campbell and J. E. Turner, "Debunking the Myth of Exercise-Induced Immune Suppression: Redefining the Impact of Exercise on Immunological Health Across the Life Span," *Frontiers in Immunology* 9 (2018): 648.

Chapter 6

1 S. Cassidy, B. Roche, D. Colbert, I. Stewart, and I. M. Grey, "A Relational Frame Skills Training Intervention to Increase General Intelligence and Scholastic Aptitude," *Learning and Individual Differences* 47 (2016): 222–235.

D. Colbert, I. Tyndall, B. Roche, and S. Cassidy, "Can SMART Training Really Increase Intelligence? A Replication Study," *Journal of Behavioral Education* 27 (2018): 509–531.

2 M. Widmann, A. M. Nieß, and B. Munz, "Physical Exercise and Epigenetic Modifications in Skeletal Muscle," *Sports Medicine* 49 (2019): 509–523.

P. Kaliman, "Epigenetics and Meditation," *Current Opinion in Psychology* 28 (2019): 76–80.

E. Jablonka and M. Lamb, *Evolution in Four Dimensions: Genetic, Epigenetic, Behavioral, and Symbolic Variation in the History of Life* (Cambridge, MA: MIT Press, 2006).

3 J. Ciarrochi, P. Parker, T. B. Kashdan, P. C. L. Heaven, and E. Barkus, "Hope and Emotional Well-Being: A Six-Year Study to Distinguish Antecedents, Correlates, and Consequences," *Journal of Positive Psychology* 10 (2015): 520–532.

C. R. Snyder, S. T. Michael, and J. S. Cheavens, "Hope as a Psychotherapeutic Foundation of Common Factors, Placebos, and Expectancies," in *The Heart and Soul of Change: What Works in Therapy*, vol. 462, ed. M. A. Hubble (Washington, DC: American Psychological Association, 1999), 179–200.

4 E. Miller, A. Rudman, N. Högman, and P. Gustavsson, "Mindset Interventions in Academic Settings: A Review," Karolinska Institutet, Report B (2016).

D. S. Yeager, et al., "A National Experiment Reveals Where a Growth Mindset Improves Achievement," *Nature* 573 (2019): 364–369.

D. S. Yeager and C. S. Dweck, "Mindsets That Promote Resilience: When Students Believe That Personal Characteristics Can Be Developed," *Educational Psychology* 47 (2012): 302–314.

5   L. Yu, S. Norton, and L. M. McCracken, "Change in 'Self-as-Context' ('Perspective-Taking') Occurs in Acceptance and Commitment Therapy for People with Chronic Pain and Is Associated with Improved Functioning," *Journal of Pain* 18 (2017): 664–672.

N. Carrasquillo and R. D. Zettle, "Comparing a Brief Self-as-Context Exercise to Control-Based and Attention Placebo Protocols for Coping with Induced Pain," *Psychological Record* 64 (2014): 659–669.

M. Foody, Y. Barnes-Holmes, D. Barnes-Holmes, L. Rai, and C. Luciano, "An Empirical Investigation of the Role of Self, Hierarchy, and Distinction in a Common Act Exercise," *Psychological Record* 65 (2015): 231–243.

6   C. M. Mueller and C. S. Dweck, "Praise for Intelligence Can Undermine Children's Motivation and Performance," *Journal of Personality and Social Psychology* 75 (1998): 33–52.

7   R. H. Smith, W. G. Parrott, E. F. Diener, R. H. Hoyle, and S. H. Kim, "Dispositional Envy," *Personality and Social Psychology Bulletin* 25 (1999): 1007–1020.

8   J. C. Hutchinson, T. Sherman, N. Martinovic, and G. Tenenbaum, "The Effect of Manipulated Self-Efficacy on Perceived and Sustained Effort," *Journal of Applied Sport Psychology* 20 (2008): 457–472.

J. Ciarrochi, P. C. L. Heaven, and F. Davies, "The Impact of Hope, Self-Esteem, and Attributional Style on Adolescents' School Grades and Emotional Well-Being: A Longitudinal Study," *Journal of Research in Personality* 41 (2007): 1161–1178.

A. W. Blanchfield, J. Hardy, H. M. De Morree, W. Staiano, and S. M. Marcora, "Talking Yourself Out of Exhaustion: The Effects of Self-Talk on Endurance Performance," *Medicine & Science in Sports & Exercise* 46 (2014): 998–1007.

Chapter 7

1   J. Montero-Marin, et al., "Self-Compassion and Cultural Values: A Cross-Cultural Study of Self-Compassion Using a Multitrait-Multimethod (MTMM) Analytical Procedure," *Frontiers in Psychology* 9 (2018): 2638.

2   P. Gilbert, K. McEwan, M. Matos, and A. Rivis, "Fears of Compassion: Development of Three Self-Report Measures," *Psychology and Psychotherapy* 84 (2011): 239–255.

3   J. A. Bailey, K. G. Hill, S. Oesterle, and J. D. Hawkins, "Parenting Practices and Problem Behavior Across Three Generations: Monitoring, Harsh Discipline, and Drug Use in the Intergenerational Transmission of Externalizing Behavior," *Developmental Psychology* 45 (2009): 1214–1226.

K. E. Williams and J. Ciarrochi, "Perceived Parenting Styles and Values Development: A Longitudinal Study of Adolescents and Emerging Adults," *Journal of Research on Adolescence* 30 (2020): 541–558.

P. C. L. Heaven and J. Ciarrochi, "Parental Styles, Gender, and the Development of Hope and Self-Esteem," *European Journal of Personality* 22 (2008): 707–724.

4   S. L. Marshall, P. D. Parker, J. Ciarrochi, and P. C. L. Heaven, "Is Self-Esteem a Cause or Consequence of Social Support? A 4-Year Longitudinal Study," *Child Development* 85 (2014): 1275–1291.

5   M. R. Leary, E. B. Tate, C. E. Adams, A. B. Allen, and J. Hancock, "Self-Compassion and Reactions to Unpleasant Self-Relevant Events: The Implications of Treating Oneself Kindly," *Journal of Personality and Social Psychology* 92 (2007): 887–904.

J. G. Breines and S. Chen, "Self-Compassion Increases Self-Improvement Motivation," *Personality and Social Psychology Bulletin* 38 (2012): 1133–1143.

6   K. R. Merikangas, et al., "Lifetime Prevalence of Mental Disorders in U.S. Adolescents: Results from the National Comorbidity Survey Replication—Adolescent Supplement (NCS-A)," *Journal of the American Academy of Child and Adolescent Psychiatry* 49 (2010): 980–989.

H. Baumeister and M. Härter, "Prevalence of Mental Disorders Based on General Population Surveys," *Social Psychiatry and Psychiatric Epidemiology* 42 (2007): 537–546.

7   A. Perkonigg, R. C. Kessler, S. Storz, and H. U. Wittchen, "Traumatic Events and Post-Traumatic Stress Disorder in the Community: Prevalence, Risk Factors and Comorbidity," *Acta Psychiatrica Scandinavica* 101 (2000): 46–59.

8 C. S. M. Ng and V. C. W. Chan, "Prevalence of Workplace Bullying and Risk Groups in Chinese Employees in Hong Kong," *International Journal of Environmental Research and Public Health* 18 (2021).

I. Chatziioannidis, F. G. Bascialla, P. Chatzivalsama, F. Vouzas, and G. Mitsiakos. "Prevalence, Causes and Mental Health Impact of Workplace Bullying in the Neonatal Intensive Care Unit Environment," *BMJ Open* 8, e018766 (2018): 329.

9 "Inequality, Poverty Rate," OECDiLibrary (2017), doi:10.1787/0fe1315d-en.

10 J. True, *Violence Against Women: What Everyone Needs to Know* (Oxford, UK: Oxford University Press, 2020).

11 R. Sheppard, F. P. Deane, and J. Ciarrochi, "Unmet Need for Professional Mental Health Care Among Adolescents with High Psychological Distress," *Australia and New Zealand Journal of Psychiatry* 52 (2018): 59–67.

D. Rickwood, F. P. Deane, C. J. Wilson, and J. Ciarrochi, "Young People's Help-Seeking for Mental Health Problems," *Australian e-Journal for the Advancement of Mental Health* 4 (2005): 218–251.

12 D. Azar, K. Ball, J. Salmon, and V. Cleland, "The Association Between Physical Activity and Depressive Symptoms in Young Women: A Review," *Mental Health and Physical Activity* 1 (2008): 82–88.

L. Christensen, "The Effect of Food Intake on Mood," *Clinical Nutrition* 20 (2001): 161–166.

M. Haack and J. M. Mullington, "Sustained Sleep Restriction Reduces Emotional and Physical Well-Being," *Pain* 119 (2005): 56–64.

T. Cullen, G. Thomas, A. J. Wadley, and T. Myers, "The Effects of a Single Night of Complete and Partial Sleep Deprivation on Physical and Cognitive Performance: A Bayesian Analysis," *Journal of Sports Sciences* 37 (2019): 2726–2734.

J. L. Etnier and Y.-K. Chang, "Exercise, Cognitive Function, and the Brain: Advancing Our Understanding of Complex Relationships," *Journal of Sport and Health Science* 8 (2019): 299–300.

Chapter 8

1 C. D. Güss, H. Devore Edelstein, A. Badibanga, and S. Bartow, "Comparing Business Experts and Novices in Complex Problem Solving," *Journal of Intelligence* 5 (2017): 20.

H. L. Dreyfus, S. E. Dreyfus, and T. Athonasiou, "Five Steps from Novice to Expert," in *Mind Over Machine: The Power of Human Intuition and Expertise in the Era of the Computer* (New York: The Free Press, 1986), 16–51.

2 Y. A. Chang and D. M. Lane, "It Takes More Than Practice and Experience to Become a Chess Master: Evidence from a Child Prodigy and Adult Chess Players," *Journal of Expertise* 1 (2018): 6–34.

3 T. Farrington-Darby and J. R. Wilson, "The Nature of Expertise: A Review," *Applied Ergonomics* 37 (2006): 17–32.

K. A. Ericsson, R. T. Krampe, and C. Tesch-Römer, "The Role of Deliberate Practice in the Acquisition of Expert Performance," *Psychological Review* 100 (1993): 363–406.

4 L. Blaine Kyllo and D. M. Landers, "Goal Setting in Sport and Exercise: A Research Synthesis to Resolve the Controversy," *Journal of Sport and Exercise Psychology* 17 (1995): 117–137.

5 W. T. Gallwey, *The Inner Game of Tennis: The Ultimate Guide to the Mental Side of Peak Performance* (New York: Pan Macmillan, 2014).

6 A. Hatzigeorgiadis and S. J. H. Biddle, "Assessing Cognitive Interference in Sport: Development of the Thought Occurrence Questionnaire for Sport," *Anxiety, Stress and Coping* 13 (2000): 65–86.

7 M. Noetel, J. Ciarrochi, B. Van Zanden, and C. Lonsdale, "Mindfulness and Acceptance Approaches to Sporting Performance Enhancement: A Systematic Review," *International Review of Sport and Exercise Psychology* 12 (2019): 139–175.

A. T. Latinjak, A. Hatzigeorgiadis, N. Comoutos, and J. Hardy, "Speaking Clearly . . . 10 Years On: The Case for an Integrative Perspective of Self-Talk in Sport," *Sport, Exercise, and Performance Psychology* 8 (2019): 353–367.

A. Hatzigeorgiadis, "Assessing Cognitive Interference in Sport."

Chapter 9

1 S. C. Hayes, K. D. Strosahl, and K. G. Wilson, *Acceptance and Commitment Therapy, Second Edition: The Process and Practice of Mindful Change* (New York: Guilford Press, 2016).

2 B. K. Hölzel, et al., "Mindfulness Practice Leads to Increases in Regional Brain Gray Matter Density," *Psychiatry Research* 191 (2011): 36–43.

T. Singer and V. Engert, "It Matters What You Practice: Differential Training Effects on Subjective Experience, Behavior, Brain and Body in the ReSource Project," *Current Opinion in Psychology* 28 (2019): 151–158.

3 R. Purser, *McMindfulness: How Mindfulness Became the New Capitalist Spirituality* (London: Repeater Books, 2019).

4 D. Rinpoche, *Great Perfection: Outer and Inner Preliminaries* (Boston: Shambhala Publications, 2008).

5 P. Khandro, https://www.pemakhandro.org.

6 DNA-V International, https://dnav.international.

7 Rinpoche, *Great Perfection.*

Part 3

1 M. Haig, *Reasons to Stay Alive* (Edinburgh, UK: Canongate Books, 2016), 181–182.

2 J. Holt-Lunstad, T. B. Smith, M. Baker, T. Harris, and D. Stephenson, "Loneliness and Social Isolation as Risk Factors for Mortality: A Meta-Analytic Review," *Perspectives on Psychological Science* 10 (2015): 227–237.

3 A. M. Grant, *Give and Take: A Revolutionary Approach to Success* (New York: Penguin, 2013).

Chapter 10

1 M. D. Ainsworth, M. Blehar, E. Waters, and S. Wall, *Patterns of Attachment: A Psychological Study of the Strange Situation* (Hillsdale, NJ: Erlbaum, 1978).

2 R. C. Fraley, "Attachment Stability from Infancy to Adulthood: Meta-Analysis and Dynamic Modeling of Developmental Mechanisms," *Personality and Social Psychology Review* 6 (2002): 123–151.

J. E. Opie, et al., "Early Childhood Attachment Stability and Change: A Meta-Analysis," *Attachment & Human Development* (2020): 1–34.

K. Bartholomew, "Avoidance of Intimacy: An Attachment Perspective," *Journal of Social and Personal Relationships* 7 (1990): 147–178.

3   K. Bartholomew and L. M. Horowitz, "Attachment Styles Among Young Adults: A Test of a Four-Category Model," *Journal of Personality and Social Psychology* 61 (1991): 226–244.

Chapter 11

1   M. D. Lieberman, *Social: Why Our Brains Are Wired to Connect* (Oxford, UK: Oxford University Press, 2013).

2   J. A. Coan, S. Kasle, A. Jackson, H. S. Schaefer, and R. J. Davidson, "Mutuality and the Social Regulation of Neural Threat Responding," *Attachment & Human Development* 15 (2013): 303–315.

3   G. E. Vaillant, "Natural History of Male Psychological Health: The Relation of Choice of Ego Mechanisms of Defense to Adult Adjustment," *Archives of General Psychiatry* 33 (1976): 535–545.

4   J. Holt-Lunstad, T. B. Smith, and J. B. Layton, "Social Relationships and Mortality Risk: A Meta-Analytic Review," *PLoS Medicine* 7 (2010): e1000316.

J. Holt-Lunstad, T. B. Smith, M. Baker, T. Harris, and D. Stephenson, "Loneliness and Social Isolation as Risk Factors for Mortality: A Meta-Analytic Review," *Perspectives on Psychological Science* 10 (2015): 227–237.

H. Dittmar, R. Bond, M. Hurst, and T. Kasser, "The Relationship Between Materialism and Personal Well-Being: A Meta-Analysis," *Journal of Personality and Social Psychology* 107 (2014): 879–924.

5   Dittmar, "The Relationship Between Materialism and Personal Well-Being."

P. Steel, V. Taras, K. Uggerslev, and F. Bosco, "The Happy Culture: A Theoretical, Meta-Analytic, and Empirical Review of the Relationship Between Culture and Wealth and Subjective Well-Being," *Personality and Social Psychology Review* 22 (2018): 128–169.

6   P. D. Parker, et al., "Hope, Friends, and Subjective Well-Being: A Social Network Approach to Peer Group Contextual Effects," *Child Development* 86 (2015): 642–650.

P. Chi, et al., "Well-Being Contagion in the Family: Transmission of Happiness and Distress Between Parents and Children," *Child Indicators Research* 12 (2019): 2189–2202.

T. Bastiampillai, S. Allison, and S. Chan, "Is Depression Contagious? The Importance of Social Networks and the Implications of Contagion Theory," *Australia and New Zealand Journal of Psychiatry* 47 (2013): 299–303.

J. Chancellor, K. Layous, S. Margolis, and S. Lyubomirsky, "Clustering by Well-Being in Workplace Social Networks: Homophily and Social Contagion," *Emotion* 17 (2017): 1166–1180.

D. Stück, H. T. Hallgrímsson, G. Ver Steeg, A. Epasto, and L. Foschini, "The Spread of Physical Activity Through Social Networks," *Proceedings of the 26th International Conference on World Wide Web* (2017): 519–528.

7 J. Donne, *John Donne: Selections from Divine Poems, Sermons, Devotions, and Prayers* (Mahwah, NJ: Paulist Press, 1990).

8 J. Ciarrochi, et al., "When Empathy Matters: The Role of Sex and Empathy in Close Friendships," *Journal of Personality* 85 (2017): 494–504.

E. C. J. Long, J. J. Angera, S. J. Carter, M. Nakamoto, and M. Kalso, "Understanding the One You Love: A Longitudinal Assessment of an Empathy Training Program for Couples in Romantic Relationships," *Family Relations* 48 (1999): 235–242.

9 B. Sahdra, J. Ciarrochi, P. D. Parker, S. Marshall, and P. C. L. Heaven, "Empathy and Nonattachment Independently Predict Peer Nominations of Prosocial Behavior of Adolescents," *Frontiers in Psychology* 6 (2015): 263.

10 A. C. Rumble, P. A. M. Van Lange, and C. D. Parks, "The Benefits of Empathy: When Empathy May Sustain Cooperation in Social Dilemmas," *European Journal of Social Psychology* 40 (2010): 856–866.

11 P. Khando, "Empathy Training," Buddhist Studies Institute (2020). For in-depth empathy training, see https://buddhiststudiesinstitute.org/courses/empathy-training.

12 Khando, "Empathy Training."

Chapter 12

1   J.-P. Sartre, *No Exit and Three Other Plays* (New York: Vintage Books, 1949).

2   K. D. Williams and S. A. Nida, "Ostracism: Consequences and Coping," *Current Directions in Psychological Science* 20 (2011): 71–75.

3   V. A. Ferreira, "Workplace Incivility: A Literature Review," *International Journal of Workplace Health Management* 13 (2020): 513–542.

    A. Gewirtz-Meydan and R. Finzi-Dottan, "Narcissism and Relationship Satisfaction from a Dyadic Perspective: The Mediating Role of Psychological Aggression," *Marriage & Family Review* 54 (2018): 296–312.

    J. Ciarrochi, B. K. Sahdra, P. H. Hawley, and E. K. Devine, "The Upsides and Downsides of the Dark Side: A Longitudinal Study into the Role of Prosocial and Antisocial Strategies in Close Friendship Formation," *Frontiers in Psychology* 10 (2019): 114.

4   N. J. S. Day, M. E. Bourke, M. L. Townsend, and B. F. S. Grenyer, "Pathological Narcissism: A Study of Burden on Partners and Family," *Journal of Personality Disorders* 34 (2020): 799–813.

    A. Tokarev, A. R. Phillips, D. J. Hughes, and P. Irwing, "Leader Dark Traits, Workplace Bullying, and Employee Depression: Exploring Mediation and the Role of the Dark Core," *Journal of Abnormal Psychology* 126 (2017): 911–920.

5   R. M. Ryan and E. L. Deci, *Self-Determination Theory: Basic Psychological Needs in Motivation, Development, and Wellness* (New York: Guilford, 2017).

Chapter 13

1   IPCC, *Climate Change 2021: The Physical Science Basis. Contribution of Working Group I to the Sixth Assessment Report of the Intergovernmental Panel on Climate Change* (Cambridge, UK: Cambridge University Press, 2021).

2   World Health Organization, et al., "International Decade for Action 'Water for Life,' 2005–2015," *Weekly Epidemiological Record* 80 (2005): 195–200.

3   M. E. Levin, M. J. Hildebrandt, J. Lillis, and S. C. Hayes, "The Impact of Treatment Components Suggested by the Psychological Flexibility Model: A Meta-Analysis of Laboratory-Based Component Studies," *Behavior Therapy* 43 (2012): 741–756.

4 P. Hawken, *Regeneration: Ending the Climate Crisis in One Generation* (London: Penguin UK, 2021).

5 D. Gameau, *2040: A Handbook for the Regeneration* (Sydney, AU: Pan Macmillan Australia, 2019).

6 K. Raworth, *Doughnut Economics: Seven Ways to Think Like a 21st-Century Economist* (White River Junction, VT: Chelsea Green Publishing, 2017).

7 M. A. Musick and J. Wilson, "Volunteering and Depression: The Role of Psychological and Social Resources in Different Age Groups," *Social Science & Medicine* 56 (2003): 259–269.

8 N. Morrow-Howell, S.-I. Hong, and F. Tang, "Who Benefits from Volunteering? Variations in Perceived Benefits," *Gerontologist* 49 (2009): 91–102.

9 K. Nairn, "Learning from Young People Engaged in Climate Activism: The Potential of Collectivizing Despair and Hope," *Young Children* 27 (2019): 435–450.

10 J. W. Kanter, et al., "What Is Behavioral Activation? A Review of the Empirical Literature," *Clinical Psychology Review* 30 (2010): 608–620.

11 D. S. Wilson, *This View of Life: Completing the Darwinian Revolution* (New York: Knopf Doubleday Publishing Group, 2019).

12 E. Barclay and B. Resnick, "How Big Was the Global Climate Strike? 4 Million People, Activists Estimate," *Vox*, September 22, 2019.

13 Extinction Rebellion, *This Is Not a Drill: An Extinction Rebellion Handbook* (London: Penguin UK, 2019).

14 "Australian Teenagers' Climate Change Class Action Case Opens 'Big Crack in the Wall,' Expert Says," ABC News Australia, May 26, 2021, https://www .abc.net.au/news/2021-05-27/climate-class-action-teenagers-vickery-coal -mine-legal-precedent/100169398.

15 IPCC, *Climate Change* (2021).

"The Economics of Climate," *Finance & Development* 56 (2019): 1–65, https://www.imf.org/external/pubs/ft/fandd/2019/12/pdf/fd1219.pdf.

16 L. W. Coyne, "Poem at the End of the World" (2021).

Louise L. Hayes, PhD, is an international acceptance and commitment therapy (ACT) trainer, speaker, clinical psychologist, and researcher collaborating on interventions for adults and young people. Hayes has published research trials using ACT, and is coauthor of *The Thriving Adolescent*—the book that introduced DNA-V—plus the best-selling books *Your Life Your Way* and *Get Out of Your Mind and Into Your Life for Teens*.

Joseph V. Ciarrochi, PhD, is a professor at the Institute for Positive Psychology and Education at Australian Catholic University. He has published more than 140 scientific journal articles and many books, including the widely acclaimed *Emotional Intelligence in Everyday Life* and *The Weight Escape*. Ciarrochi has been honored with more than four million dollars in research funding. His work has been discussed on TV and radio, and in magazines and newspaper articles. He is ranked in the top 2 percent of scientists in the world across all disciplines.

Ann Bailey, MPsych, is an experienced ACT practitioner and supervisor who developed an award-winning public mental health service for the treatment of borderline personality disorder (BPD) and anxiety disorders—integrating ACT, cognitive behavioral therapy (CBT), and dialectical behavior therapy (DBT). Ann supervises a team of clinicians as director of her ACT-based Anxiety and Stress Clinic.

Illustrator **Katharine Hall** is based in Wellington, New Zealand. From her wonderful studio in Aotearoa, she tells stories that can translate across languages—specializing in ink work and digital designs for individuals, start-ups, and businesses both big and small.

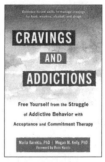
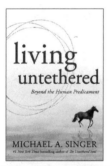
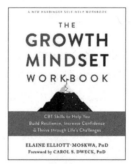